UNSTOPPABLE PROSPERITY

LEARN THE INVESTMENT STRATEGY
I'VE USED TO BEAT THE MARKET EVERY YEAR

by Charles Payne

Unstoppable Prosperity
Learn the Strategy I've Used to Beat the Market Every Year

Unstoppable Prosperity
351 W. Washington St.
Kearney, MO 64060
1-800-296-9890
support@UnstoppableProsperity.com

Cover Design by Paradigm Direct, LLC

Internal Design by Jeffective Design & Illustration

Published by Paradigm Direct, LLC

Printed in the United States of America

First Edition

Hardcover Book ISBN: 978-1-7329113-4-5
Paperback Book ISBN: 978-1-7329113-3-8

There can be no unstoppable prosperity without unstoppable love, unstoppable support and unstoppable inspiration.

Thanks to my wife Yvonne for being all those things and so much more.

TABLE OF CONTENTS

INTRODUCTION

Imagine the feeling of waking up each day excited, knowing you have the money to make your dreams come true; even those dreams you wouldn't allow yourself to believe could ever happen.

How great would it be to live with the confidence that you're prepared, no matter what financial challenges you face. Worries of outliving your money never cross your mind. You're even able to help the ones you love and support causes and charities so you can pay forward your success.

That, my friends, is the feeling of *Unstoppable Prosperity*. I've been blessed to achieve it in life, and I want you to have it too. So, what does it take to get there and stay there? It's more than just initially reaching the summit of a mountain. You want to be able to stay at the peak. Ultimately, I want you to be able to build a home and live there!

The great news is getting there, and staying there, require the same exact tools and commitment.

Even better news is that these tools are available to anyone who has the commitment to use them.

In fact, the biggest hurdle and first step in this journey is understanding that this opportunity is available for anyone, especially you. You must stop thinking and saying you're at a dead end, because you aren't. Of course, there are things you'll have to adjust in your life to achieve Unstoppable Prosperity. But those adjustments are very doable.

From the moment you awake to the moment you go to sleep, you're fueling wealth for others. I want to show you how you can take advantage of the greatest money-making machine in history to grow your *own* wealth and increase your *own* financial security.

There are a lot of combinations of approaches to get on the road to financial independence and they all involve a real game plan, discipline and commitment that eventually allows your hard-earned dollars to work for you. The central key is to have your money increasing in value faster than the rate of inflation and faster than those slow-moving, low-expectation, pedestrian investment plans that Wall Street sells to you but would never accept in their own portfolios.

What you'll find in this book is not a get rich quick scheme. Rather, you'll find a way of building wealth in a timely fashion to change your life and secure your family's future.

The secret is having and attaining knowledge, not hunches. The key ingredient is doing the work, not waving some magic wand. You can win the jackpot but it's not instantaneous and it's not luck.

Owning great businesses is the way to building wealth. When you read any list of the richest people, other than dictators and sultans, all are based on ownership in great businesses. Why aren't you an owner of those businesses?

That's why the stock market is the greatest wealth creation machine ever devised. You can own the same businesses that the richest people in the world own. You won't own as much as the billionaires, which is why we ride the inevitable waves of the market differently. But the important thing to realize is that the market offers everyone, including *you*, tremendous opportunities.

THE MARKET IS NOT EFFICIENT OR A PERFECT HARBINGER

Of course, if it were just a matter of putting money into any old stock, everyone would do it. The key to creating Unstoppable Prosperity is in picking the right stocks, at the right time. Remember, as you put your money to work, your goal is to outperform the market over the long term and, certainly, those plain vanilla retirement plans that've been spinning their wheels. You already have the advantage of untapped knowledge but have lacked the faith to take action.

In this book you'll learn to take what you already know, including great instincts, and couple it with information, historical knowledge and my proven techniques. This combination will give you the leverage to change your current economic trajectory.

NO DART-THROWING

There's a school of thought that the market is efficient because there's a tremendous amount of information available and it's built into the day-to-day prices. Wow, that's spectacularly incorrect. I wish it was that simple. If it were, we wouldn't see individual stocks and markets make crazy, double-digit moves in a single session. There wouldn't be so many "surprises" and the market wouldn't rely so much on "consensus" thinking. I'll explain more about this later in the book.

Right now, it's critical to realize that big market declines don't always signal an impending recession and big upside moves can be driven more by fear of missing out - ignoring all that free information swirling in the universe.

The reality is there are a lot of great resources out there for investors. However, too many people, including the "experts," rely on others to **maybe** read the information and then **maybe** interpret that information properly. I want to cut out the middlemen of information because they're wrong too often. Besides that, their motivation and goals are probably different than yours. I wrote this book to help you learn the skills you need to confidently make your own investment decisions.

TIME TO FIX YOUR APPROACH

If you're already in the stock market, there's a 95% chance you're going about it the wrong way. I don't mean that as an insult. It's an observation based on my decades of working with a wide range of investors.

I've found most mistakes can be put into two general categories. The first revolves around a desire to beat the market on a day-to-day basis. The second is on the other end of the spectrum. It involves blindly pouring money into investment schemes that work out a lot better in the brochure or academic study but not so well in real-life wealth building. Both of these mistakes have left millions of people far behind in their investing goals.

If you're already active in the market and honest with yourself, you know there needs to be changes to your approach. For some, it could be minor tweaks. For others, it means ripping everything up. The *key* is to understand what those changes need to be and then **take action**.

The fact you're reading this book tells me you want to make some adjustments or are considering becoming a stock market investor. In other words, you want to **take action**. I've worked hard in this book to show you how to rely on and measure observable fundamental, technical and even behavioral trends for long-term success.

The best part is *you* will control your own destiny.

The purpose of this book is to help you get over your anxieties and fears of the stock market while also giving you the tools that will empower you to navigate pitfalls rather than falling victim to them. Ironically, it's the latter that cures the former. It's only natural, we're all more confident when we know what we're doing.

The more you're able to assess conditions and focus on facts rather than the noise, the less afraid you'll be and the fewer mistakes you'll commit.

I'm going to teach you the exact same investing approach and strategy that's allowed me to beat the market over the last 12 years - through some of the market's toughest times and some of the best of times.

Now, this isn't a promise that you'll always be able to do what I do or implement the strategies perfectly. The idea is more to allow you to see how I invest so that you can learn the reasoning behind the investments I take.

The most important part is for you to learn how to identify the difference between strong and weak investments. With this knowledge, you should be able to better identify the factors that are consistent with successful investments and attempt to avoid those factors which are commonly found in losers.

I encourage you to check out my investing results at **www.unstoppableprosperity.com/paynesresults**. This page displays the results of my primary alert service for the past 12 years.

As you may expect, every investment is not a winner but the majority of them are. Part of my strategy is to keep my losses to a minimum so my winners can overcompensate for inevitable losses. This balance has been one of the keys in helping me to obtain Unstoppable Prosperity.

Of course, all investments or strategies that I used to achieve these results may not be suitable for you, your particular investment objectives, financial situation or needs. I'll teach you my strategies so you can determine what is the most appropriate for you.

My approach has evolved over three decades, so you have the benefit of learning from the mistakes I made. My net worth has ranged from zero to $275 million. My goal is that by the end of this book, you'll understand my approach and be able to apply that approach to your own investing.

There are **three pillars** to my approach that consider key aspects that move stocks and markets:

- Fundamental Analysis
- Technical Analysis
- Behavioral Analysis

These Pillars, and my unique approach to them, is what has given my success in the markets the structural integrity to weather any storm, to beat the market in good times and bad.

Right now, too many investors conflate genius with luck during raging bull markets and too many follow the herd off a cliff during crushing bear markets. The irony is when people are getting lucky on the way up, they do less research and less work necessary for sustained long-term success. I want to help you avoid that error.

Another error is that of procrastination. Without doing the work, an investor can feel unsure about making a move, and for some that could mean not getting into the market at all. Allowing procrastination to extend even longer means postponing or never attaining the real game plan you need.

My biggest goal is to give you confidence in your own ability. With my strategy you'll confidently enter every trade with a plan. You'll know exactly why you're buying each stock and have a predetermined exit strategy. I don't subscribe to or teach the "buy and hope it goes up" theory. I believe every trade should be calculated.

I don't want to imply that this will be all sunshine and lollipops. Losses will happen. But I'll show you how to minimize them and remove the emotions that cause novice investors to make costly knee jerk reactions. I've been able to consistently make more than the market in good times and lose less than the market in bad times. That is how you create *Unstoppable Prosperity*.

I don't want you to think of taking a loss as something to be ashamed of or a reason to fold your tent and walk away. Mostly, taking losses should never engender sulking and protest. Losses should be lessons learned that allow for bigger gains in the future. Likewise, I don't want you to be content with modest gains all the time. Using my Three Pillars I'll present, you'll be able to understand when to take profits and when to hold a position.

Interestingly, over the years I've found that for many investors, "ringing the cash register" is sometimes harder than taking a loss. This odd contradiction is a natural human reaction and perhaps the most damaging of all self-inflicted wounds. To overcome deeply embedded mistakes and these natural human reactions, I need you to have confidence, make the commitment and then execute.

I believe as you read this book and incorporate the methodology presented, hurdles will be lowered and the things that caused defeat will become the opportunities they often are. From here on out we're partners. This book is an analytical tool that allows me to weigh in and help whenever you need it.

ROOTING FOR THE UNDERDOG

Throughout this book, you'll learn about my backstory and personal journey that brought me from the depths of poverty to where I am today.

I had a very unique childhood of seeing the world and, for a time, didn't know of economic distress. My early years of living on Army bases around the world provided personal comfort but blindness to more dire economic conditions.

That all changed when I arrived in Harlem at age 12. Back then Harlem was, perhaps, the most dangerous and impoverished neighborhood in America. I hadn't thought about money a day in my life until we had none. I never thought about empty cupboards until ours were empty. I never thought about heat and hot water until we had none.

We were living in absolute poverty.

Living on army bases in the 1960s and early 1970s not only shielded me from poverty and other societal ills, like racism and violence, but also from hopelessness and frustration. My awakening is why I live my life to help others, especially those that face the tallest hurdles and have the greatest degree of hopelessness.

Growing up in Harlem, I saw people, especially women, getting up before the sun, making breakfast, getting children ready for school and then rushing off in crowded streets and dirty subways to get to a job that paid crumbs. No matter how hard they worked, they still lived in the same building and neighborhood as the few people that didn't work and settled for government assistance. These hard-working people couldn't get ahead but they kept pushing forward every day.

Why didn't those parents, including my own mother, throw in the towel and settle for welfare? It broke my heart and simultaneously sparked something inside me that I carry to this day. The desire to help people willing to work hard find ways out of their circumstances, to change the arc of their lives for their children.

I was the oldest in our family. As the oldest, I was thrust into the position of helping my family survive. So, I began working odd jobs and odd hustles like cleaning car windshields at traffic lights, packing groceries and shoveling snow for business store fronts.

But I knew I needed more. Like any red-blooded American, I equated the stock market with wealth and, although I had always heard it was an exclusive club, I was determined to get involved. I had no choice.

What might seem like a handicap to some turned out to be a real advantage to me. You see, I couldn't afford to hire someone to train me, so I had to learn everything on my own. It was harder back then, long before the internet and financial media. I taught myself how to read the Wall Street Journal at age 14 and told my mother I would work on Wall Street one day.

I bought my first mutual fund at age 17. I was so young my mother had to co-sign the paperwork. After a few years of ups and downs, including a grand slam with my very first stock purchase (I bought MCI after reading about the maverick founder stringing together rooftop antennas to take on communications giants), I came to realize the greatest asset wasn't money or access. It was **knowledge**.

It reminds me of an old joke I heard a lot when I first began working on Wall Street:

> *Q.* How do you make a million dollars in the stock market?

> *A.* Start with two million.

Knowledge is the secret that puts the lie to that old joke.

Knowledge allows investors to escape costly and woefully underperforming investment schemes and managers that get paid no matter how poor their performance. Knowledge allows you to be opportunistic when you might have otherwise made costly mistakes. Knowledge allows for mitigating mistakes and maximizing gains, which speeds up the process of building wealth. Knowledge allows you to position yourself for Unstoppable Prosperity.

Heck, you already know in your own industry the difference that various levels of knowledge play in separating the best from the also-rans.

My approach is a Rosetta Stone for continued learning because Unstoppable Prosperity means never stopping the learning or understanding of the businesses you own. The world will open up to you and you'll be empowered to connect the dots. You'll have the chance to explore natural curiosities and the stuff you already know but never had the confidence, or tools, to assess and use to make money through skillful investing.

Let's call it your epiphany.

MY EPIPHANY

When I told my mother, at age 14, that I would work on Wall Street, she never doubted that I would... but nobody else thought I could make it. Most of the people I knew, from friends and neighbors to my teachers, dismissed my "silly talk." Many even laughed in my face. I taught myself to read the Wall Street Journal and other publications I would find discarded by those who could afford to buy them. I romanticized a Wall Street that I later learned didn't exist in real life.

My first job was at EF Hutton analyzing trades made by various desks.

Reviewing those trades was boring, but not the size of those trades and not the access to the people in various departments tasked with making those trades. I saw recklessness, especially by those with the greatest connections to the "C suites." I saw tribalism, which could've engendered greater competition but only created inefficacies.

But for a young man pinching himself at working on Wall Street, I mostly saw the passions of investment professionals in their own abilities and knowledge. Fortunately for me, they all loved to share it with this young, wide-eyed kid who asked a lot of questions. It was a great place to learn about macro influences on micro outcomes. It was like going to college but instead of theories, I saw real-life outcomes.

However, there was a "fly in the ointment." The problem was I wasn't making much money. When I got the phone call that I got the job, my wife and one-year old daughter and I were living in a room inside an apartment in one of the roughest neighborhoods in New York. So, when I got that call, it was one of the greatest moments of my life. The $13,000 annual salary was the most money I had ever earned. It would allow me to move into an apartment rather than renting a room that barely had space for the pullout sofa.

I was elated to get this job. But my financial dreams had no limitations. So, after a year of great learning, I wanted to move on to the next level. I got that chance when I was sponsored for the broker exam after running into an acquaintance who was a stock broker and was willing to introduce me to her manager.

Now all I had to do was pass the test. Back then it was administered once a month, typically on a Saturday.

I was working at EF Hutton and had another job doing microfilm at a large hospital so there was little extra time to prepare. The week of the test, a friend who was being sponsored by a larger firm invited me to a preparation class he was taking. That was Wednesday night. I took a few practice tests and scored in the mid-70s. One of the instructors remarked I would probably fail the test that coming Saturday.

I just smiled and thought to myself, "You don't know me."

I took the six-hour test with a couple hundred people and finished in less than three hours. Only one person finished before I did. I went to the office and told management I passed, even though the results would take a couple of weeks before officially known.

Upon becoming a broker, my view of Wall Street changed almost immediately. I came in doing my own research and selling stocks in companies I thought would change the world. The problem was the firm had stocks in inventory known as "house stocks" that paid the broker substantially more money.

It didn't take long to figure out my glamourous vision of a broker doing research and learning about individual client needs was a farce. It was just a regular salesman's job. Moreover, there was a lot more money to be made selling higher-risk house stocks rather than something like *Burroughs Welcome.* This is the stock I loved because the company was ahead of the curve with treatments for HIV-AIDS... but it wasn't a house stock.

My second full month in the business I opened more new accounts than anyone else but was denied access to hot initial public offerings for my clients because I hadn't sold any house stock. The final blow came when payday rolled around. I made significantly less money than people in the office who raised a lot less money than I had.

After that, I played the game. The day I got my first big paycheck my daughter had on the same diaper for more than 24 hours because there were none left, and we had one can of food in the cupboard. I was never happy about the situation. Eventually, I realized I needed to continue doing my own research and make my own recommendations. Recommendations that were truly in the best interests of my clients. That's what inspired me to start my own Wall Street research firm. And it was the success of that firm that got the attention of the media and eventually led to an offer to host my own show on the Fox Business Network called *"Making Money with Charles Payne."*

Many viewers ask for advice and want to know how I invest. They hear that I consistently beat the market and want to learn how they can do it too. That's what inspired me to write this book. I want to give you, and every other individual investor I can reach, the knowledge, tools and confidence you need to take charge of your investing and reap the meaningful returns you need to reach your financial goals and retirement dreams.

THE ROADMAP

In this book, I want to show you that you already have great instincts and know a lot of great potential investments but just need to learn how to take the next step and make money. Think about how many times you wish you had thought of something or owned a hot business or product. You can! You should!

You know in your heart it's true, that's why you're reading this book. But if you're like most, two things have been holding you back. The lack of having a proven investing plan you believe in, and an overabundance of fear. This book is going to knock down both of those barriers.

We'll look at the folly of using money managers who rarely beat the averages (but are happy to collect their fees anyway), owning mutual funds that never deliver as promised, and following the crowd, who might be following machines that were reacting to something someone said on financial television.

We'll look at the mistakes that sabotage your efforts – don't worry, you're not alone on these mistakes.

You'll learn to crunch the numbers at different levels and to drill down so you can decide how engaged you want to be. Whether you want to do short-term trading or long-term investing, there are step-by-step methods.

This book is for everyone - including those not actively investing in the stock market, those in the market who are ready to make a real commitment, and those with large under-performing portfolios looking to take greater control of their destiny.

Everyone deserves Unstoppable Prosperity.

I'll help you get there with what I call Payne's Principles.

1. My Three Pillars of Success

- Fundamental Analysis
- Technical Analysis
- Behavioral Analysis

2. Good Old-Fashioned Elbow Grease

As we go through each chapter, I'll give you actionable steps to shift the dynamics of your life from "you working for your money" to "your money working for you." You can decide how much work you want to put into this endeavor but forget the idea of wealth creation with no work on your part. If you take that approach, you'll only make others rich.

3. Commitment

Once you have the knowledge, you'll never be dismayed or dissuaded from being an investor again. That doesn't mean you'll always have every nickel in the market or you won't have setbacks. Remember, the names on the list of the richest people don't change much because of bear markets or occasional crashes. The truth is that those periods when most people are bailing is when the greatest money-making investment opportunities are being created. There's money to be made in every market condition. Learning how to do that is how you create Unstoppable Prosperity.

I'm pumped and excited you have this book in your hands, so let's get started.

CHAPTER

CREATING UNSTOPPABLE PROSPERITY IN A CHANGING MARKET

THIS ISN'T YOUR GRANDFATHER'S MARKET

Wall Street losing dough on every share
They're blaming it on longer hair
Big men smoking in their easy chairs
On a fat cigar without a care

"People Make the World Go Around"
~ Stylistics

It can be said that this isn't your grandfather's stock market but more than likely, your grandfather wasn't an active investor in the market. If he was an investor, it was probably because he had access through employment options which were then very rare.

When I was growing up, stock market participants came out of Central Casting. They fit the image you get when listening to the lyrics of the Stylistics classic, "People Make the World Go Around," a bunch of old dudes with long grey sideburns and big bellies to match those fat cigars.

And yes, you get the impression that even big losing days didn't faze them much or, at least, they held to the "code of conduct" that emotions couldn't betray an air of superiority. And when the market was hit too hard it was the fault of those kids with long hair upsetting society at large.

From time to time, the public made its move into the market, much to the disdain of the investing elites that always saw that as a sign to get out immediately. It's said that Joe Kennedy once stopped to get a shoeshine before heading up to the office when the shoeshine boy started with small talk.

Shoeshine boy: *"Hey Mr. Kennedy, it's a nice day for late October, right?"*

Joe Kennedy: *"It's okay."*

Shoeshine boy: *"I have to say, the day matches the year. 1929 is one we'll never forget, right?"*

Joe Kennedy: *"It's okay."*

Shoeshine boy: *"Hey Mr. Kennedy, you see those shares of Amalgamated Mining zooming?"*

Joe Kennedy: *"What?"*

Shoeshine boy: *"Amalgamated, I loaded up and think I'm going to buy more."*

Joe Kennedy: *"I must go now kid. How much? Never mind, here's a dollar."*

According to legend, on that morning, October 28, 1929, Joe Kennedy sold everything and the stock market crashed the next day.

I'm not sure how much is folklore and how much is real, but those big men, more likely to be ensconced in a mansion in Greenwich, Connecticut or a yacht in the Caribbean, are still disdainful of individual investors in the market. But today, fortunately for us, they just have to deal with it.

The Stylistics released the "People" album in 1971, the same year a young entrepreneur named Charles Schwab set up shop in San Francisco.

Now the fat cats must deal with those long-hair kids in the stock market as well as their mothers and fathers. Charles Schwab established discount trading and that set the market up on the road of democratization. Now, everyone has access to the greatest wealth-creation machine in the history of mankind.

Technology has added speed and accessibility, from anywhere at anytime, into the mix and now people really do make the stock market go around. Of course, some things never change:

Everyone wants to make a killing in the stock market.

Everyone blames someone else when they lose money.

In fact, these days, it's not uncommon for long-haired investors to blame the greedy mistakes of fat cats for losing sessions. My mission is to give you the inspiration and tools to navigate the market so it's not about rolling the dice and assigning blame.

Our goal is long-term wealth creation.

It's not a full-time job but it does require a commitment that honors your hard-earned funds. I'll give you the plan and only ask that you learn the approach and remain committed because this is a long-term endeavor.

DIFFERENT PLAYING FIELD

Those big men in the song sat around in private clubs or offices. They had special equipment and banks of telephones with operators ready to connect them in rapid fashion to information or for execution of buy and sell orders.

Handwritten notes were exchanged in coat rooms and a wink or a nod could be worth millions. There were runners that would bolt across town for the inside scoop. Sometimes people even used the postal service and mailed information (always first-class stamps).

The speed of the market has changed with the speed of communications and it's had a profound impact on the stock market - especially the advent of computer trading and algorithms. But the more things change the more they stay the same, and in the end, the cream of the crop will rise and generate the most wealth for investors.

Unfortunately, Wall Street has always attracted speculators, schemers and get-rich-quick operators. These days, they're armed with instant execution capabilities, chat room discussions, and societal interest that can spark manias and inflate bubbles in a blink of an eye.

There are times when the quick buck looks great and seems like easy money, that is until you're out of money.

When I started on Wall Street, a guy named Jack was the oldest broker in the office. He was famous for saying, "I wanna give you the edge." I loved him but there was something melancholy about him going for the quick buck at his age, more often than not, only to lose.

He played the ponies and took me to the track with him one day where he showed me his system. It made sense to me, but we didn't win. He bet on football games and knew about injury reports and other scuttlebutt that he felt gave him the edge.

He was a wonderful man, but our friendship made me worry about getting old without a nest egg and trying to hustle the system for quick bucks. I understood I needed the edge. But the one thing that I learned from so many people was that *there are no shortcuts*. I also came to understand that I better be in control of my own economic future.

Lots of people want to have it two ways. On the one hand, they're somewhat responsible for their investment decisions. On the other, they take just enough guidance from someone else so they have someone to blame if things don't work out. After every market crash, I get a lot of new clients and they all tell me their broker messed them up.

For some that's true, but for many investors, greed and an undisciplined approach messed them up. Virtually all of them had no real game plan, and many conflated luck with skill. Some knew they didn't know much but assumed the good times would never end, so why learn how to evaluate individual stocks or the stock market or manage market risk?

This isn't to say Wall Street hasn't made huge mistakes. Honestly, the negative reputation of Wall Street is well-deserved. There hasn't been a generation in America that didn't have their own Wall Street scandal. Making matters worse is that many of us had to see taxpayer funds and the Federal Reserve save Wall Street to the tune of trillions of dollars after its subprime mortgage scandal came crashing down.

But we still invest because, despite all the horror stories, the market continues to mint millionaires and change lives.

Moreover, there are hundreds of thousands of hardworking men and women in the industry trying to help investors make money in the stock market. Whether you use such help or not is fine with me, but you'd be selling yourself short by not educating yourself and having real control over your own investments.

I truly want to give you the edge.

I want to make *you* the edge.

TIME TO PAY YOURSELF

Nothing drives me crazier than when people say things like, "The market isn't for me." or "I'm not in the stock market."

Yes, you're in the market because you're in the economy and, whether you realize it or not, you're making other people rich.

From the moment you wake up, you're in the market (heck, you're in the market when you're asleep, too).

You hit an alarm clock or turn off the chiming from your smartphone or simply tell your digital assistant you're awake. All these products are probably manufactured by companies that are publicly traded. These companies rake in sales and many become so ubiquitous in our society that the founders and CEOs have become household names. Here are a few you'll most likely recognize:

- Elon Musk
- Bill Gates
- Meg Whitman
- Jeff Bezos
- Warren Buffett

I always tell the story of people coming up to me in the street to say how much they enjoy my commentary on TV and then mention they aren't in the market. I look at them and, invariably, they're wearing clothes, sneakers, hats and sunglasses. I ask about those things and generally the person is thrilled to discuss the latest fashion purchase or newest gadget.

Next, noticing their enthusiasm, I ask if they ever recommended the product (or service) to others and almost always, the answer is, "Yes."

By now I'm perplexed. I'll pose the following to them; since they're buying the product (or service) with their own hard-earned money and telling friends about it, why shouldn't they be part owners of the company? Hmm... never thought about it like that.

I'll often take it one step further and ask if they've recommended the product or service to more than five people, including family members. The answer once again is, "Yes." And still, they're either too intimidated to own shares in the company or think investing is out of their league.

The reality is that all of these non-investors are participating in the market, just limited to the "spending" side and not the "earning" side. We need to change that.

The American Dream is still alive. You can reach it, and Unstoppable Prosperity, beginning *right now*.

TAKING THE PLUNGE

It's interesting that all the terms used for investing in the market sound ominous.

> *Taking the plunge*
>
> *Rolling the dice*
>
> *Taking a shot*

Even the professional investors refer to up-sessions in the market as "risk on." That bothers me. I believe that the biggest risk anyone could take these days is growing old without investments, only relying on the government's social safety nets.

For me, when people are selling, that should be considered "risk on". Perhaps an even greater "risk" should be when they stay forever on the outside looking in, noses pressed against the glass but too afraid or intimidated to get into the mix. Of course it's intimidating, and in many ways all the tools that've been developed over the years can make it easier to make mistakes.

Sure, those fat cats from yesteryear didn't have fast trading execution, unlimited apps, and tons of free research. They were more confident in their actions, and even when they weren't, they couldn't make costly mistakes in the blink of an eye like you can today. It's not unlike power tools, if you use them incorrectly it could get messy - really quickly.

I know what you're thinking right now... "I thought he was trying to get me in the market not scare the heck out of me."

LOL. I just want to be straight with you because I know

all the mistakes you've made and all the mistakes you're going to want to make. After three decades of working with individual investors, I've seen it all and I know we need to lay our cards on the table and then move forward.

My goal is to get you to *take the plunge* with a game plan designed to teach you and provide you with tools but, ultimately, to make sure you don't betray your own goals. Everybody makes mistakes. The most seasoned, wealthy investors make mistakes. But they know how to limit their mistakes and maximize their gains. I want to show you how to do that as well.

RIDING THE WAVES

There's an old term on Wall Street about the "herd mentality" which is meant to be an insult. Conventional wisdom demeans the collective knowledge and actions of crowds acting in unison. Ironically, there's been a lot of clinical work that suggests the crowds make the best decisions. The image is a thousand shoeshine boys buying and selling at the same time.

I don't like the term *herd mentality* and I don't think it makes sense. Heck, you want to be in markets that are moving higher. Plus, I don't buy the notion that the individual investor is always wrong. I think these investors often have better instincts than professionals and many have greater knowledge of Main Street. They just lack the ability, or confidence, to leverage that knowledge.

That lack of confidence is most prevalent and dangerous when the market is selling off. Panic is the bane of investors. In the 1800s, big market moves to the downside were called panics. This is when the wave is racing toward the exits and it's everybody for themselves.

One of my biggest goals in this book is to make sure you don't fall victim to those massive waves of panic selling. In fact, we want to be able to take advantage of those waves. Ultimately, these panics reflect emotions more than a significant change in fundamentals by the time the worst is over.

Nobody is born with some kind of ice water in their veins to offset market panics. But my goal is the make sure you can ride those waves and pursue your goals - using *knowledge* and not just *emotion* - whether the market is going up or down.

INVESTING BY THE NUMBERS

These days fewer and fewer brokers know what stocks their clients own. Their job has become a constant effort to increase "assets under management" (AUM). What they manage isn't as important to them as the total dollar amount they manage. Then there are those investment funds that are supposed to deliver success, but never seem to live up to the hype.

When I refer to Wall Street's goal of AUM, that applies to all those fancy funds in your 401K or other investment programs that you have on autopilot as well.

These funds have different names and different stated goals, but all too often don't deliver the diversity or performance advertised. I'll get into greater detail later, but I think you already know what I'm talking about. In the end, these funds are often trying to "ride the wave" as much as any individual investor, and they pay the price when there's a wipe out.

My goal isn't to get you hopping around the investing world day to day looking for the "hot trade" of the moment. Conversely, you cannot move the needle on your wealth by taking too many wipeouts.

Your destiny shouldn't be in the hands of an expert who is so wedded to an approach he or she becomes more like Captain Ahab, and you're left high and dry in their elusive search for the next grand slam investment - their white whale. Often, they miss the mark and they do it with your money. I think there's a better way.

My approach is a balanced approach that strives to make money, stay nimble, but not try to game all the nuances, daily twists and turns in the stock market.

You have dreams and goals.

You want your golden years to be golden.

You want to send your children to college.

You want financial independence.

*You want **Unstoppable Prosperity**.*

INVESTING IN THE NEW MILLENNIUM

One of the reasons I've written this book is to help investors, armed with an array of information and resources of the modern world, be able to employ undeniable methods of success that harken back to a time when it was understood that success came with time and temperament.

There's a lot of information out there, but who knows how to interpret the information? Who takes the time to interpret the information? Face it, all these bells and whistles that make life easier have their limits.

I recently discovered...

I forgot how to write in cursive.

I only know a few phone numbers by memory.

Soon I'll forget how to parallel park.

We aren't talking about writing a personalized thank you note or calling up an old friend or even trying to squeeze a car into a tight parking spot. We're talking about your future.

In many aspects of our lives, we've come to rely on machines. I need you to become the machine that builds your future out of an abundance of experience. I want you to crunch numbers. You have to understand how to read income statements and balance sheets as well as understanding chart formations and volume spikes. If this is all new to you, not to worry. I'll show you what you need to know. If you have experience, I want you to take a look with "new eyes." Be more knowledgeable and critical. I'll show you what I mean.

In order to unleash the knowledge you have, and those dormant instincts you've never had confidence in, we'll leverage all the tools available to make sure you're generating the wealth you desire through my Unstoppable Prosperity game plan.

This game plan is for you whether you're already active in the market or are now ready to stop pressing your nose against the glass and come inside to reach your dreams.

There are old truisms about the stock market that never go out of style but there are new aspects of investing that are part of the modern age. You can't avoid all the pitfalls of investing in a world that sees the Dow Jones Industrial Average move hundreds of points in the blink of an eye. You can't afford to be caught flat-footed. And when you're caught off-guard, you must be able to make sure the emotions of the crowd aren't going to cost you a fortune. By the way, when I talk about the "crowd" it includes financial publications and folks on television.

You're going to hear a lot of voices telling you to panic and others telling you to chill out. Both are right, but both are wrong, and this is where it's incumbent on you to be able to take control. You're going to have to make judgements, but you'll make them based on an understanding of value, risk and history.

The people on TV don't know your goals and have never met your children. Even your broker will be lost at key moments when all hell is breaking loose. It'll come down to you and the techniques I've laid out for you in this book.

Trading is faster, information is faster and pressure to make snap decisions is greater. This is the nature of investing in the modern world. Don't let it be the reason you fail. Use it to your advantage for even greater success.

TRADERS VS. INVESTORS

There are so many terms specific to investing that people feel compelled to act like they understand or are forced to accept them as personal labels. Most investors don't have firm goals other than making money.

It's time to change that.

I always ask those new to the market if they consider themselves traders or investors and most of the time the answer is, "I just want to make money." Yes, but what's your temperament? Are you looking to make money quickly or a lot more money by allowing ideas in your portfolio to germinate a little on their way to more substantive gains?

Newcomers will often get a confused look on their faces when I ask this. After all, who doesn't want to make big money buying and holding hot stocks? Sometimes their attitude and responses change when I then ask about how much of a paper loss could they handle before they can't fall asleep at night? If the answer is, "Not much." I let them know they're going to have to become short-term traders or find a way to overcome those feelings of loss and angst when the chips are down.

By the way, I ask seasoned market participants the same question and, overwhelmingly, I get the same ubiquitous reply, "I don't know. I just want to make money."

So, what's the difference? Here's how I view the difference between a trader and an investor.

Traders

Good traders are like good poker players. They have patience, move quickly and are extremely disciplined. Thousands of would-be card sharks sign up for the World Series of Poker events and it always boils down to the same dozen or so at the last two tables.

The secret to being a great trader, or a great poker player, is the ability to take occasional losses and remain calm and focused on your plan.

Like so many terms on Wall Street, being a trader means different things to different people. Moreover, there are different types of traders, from those that trade during the day and have no positions at the closing bell, to those that hold positions for upwards of thirty-days for swing trades.

Someone we would identify as a trader is one who is looking to book profits on anything from an incremental, fractional move to three percent or more. A successful trader looks for, and executes on, the same parameters for both gains and losses.

This is where a lot of would-be traders get jammed up. The trader's gut or, as often is the case, his ego will hold him back on taking a loss. By hesitating, or going with his gut, the loss compounds and ends up being greater than his average gain. That's when he'll begin to rationalize and then that one losing trade could become large enough to erase numerous winning trades.

Being a trader is more time-consuming and mentally fatiguing then being a buy and hold investor. Yet, there's something comforting about ringing the cash register all the time. And in those times when the broad market is in trouble and all stocks are under pressure, traders can take comfort knowing they're sitting on more cash and have less exposure.

It's also easier for traders to flip directions and make trades that increase in value as the market or individual stocks lose value. Traders won't ever have the giant score of a stock that goes from $10 to $100 because he might be in and out of that stock a dozen times on the way up, possibly missing out on the biggest percentage move.

Investors

Buying and holding is the hallmark of being an investor but even that has morphed over the years. According to research, the average holding time for stocks in general has tumbled.

Average Holding Periods:

> *1960s*: *eight years four months*
>
> *1970s*: *five years three months*
>
> *1980s*: *two years nine months*
>
> *1990s*: *two years two months*
>
> *2000s*: *one year two months*
>
> *Today*: *four to eight months*

Despite the faster nature of investing, there are a lot of stocks that can be bought and held for years. Some stocks rally on hype and then collapse only to rally over a much longer period of years when the early hype finally comes to fruition. Ideally, you'd be out of the stock(s) during those lean times. An important skill is the ability to recognize the time to get back into the stock.

Just as trading can be ambiguous, defining the period during which one holds a stock to qualify as an investment can be arbitrary. I have positions I buy and hold looking for a double-digit return in three months or longer. I allow the underlying fundamentals and technicals, not the share price, to dictate how long I hold onto the stock.

Then, there are positions I buy and hold based on macro assumptions that may not influence price immediately, but I want to hold in my portfolio years from now.

Investors shouldn't fret over market gyrations and even periodic short-term pullbacks on things like the market punishing a stock because the earnings missed by a penny. By the same token, it's easy to be dishonest with yourself and rationalize that the stock will come back. If an investor uses this rationalization based on hope, rather than research, the trader has an advantage over the investor.

IDEAL APPROACH

I think the ideal scenario for investors is to have ideas that you **trade (30% of your portfolio)**, others you **buy and hold** looking for double digit returns **(60% of your portfolio)** and a few names that have the **potential to be grand slams** over a period including several years **(10% of your portfolio)**.

The secret here is to make sure to apply the same

parameters to any ideas you originally employed to create the position. I'll go into greater detail on this in Chapter 5.

WHO ARE YOU?

There are different types of people and personalities in the investing universe.

Active Investors

Cowboys and gunslingers: always looking for a giant score and willing to buy the riskiest stocks or assets. Often these investors get involved in the hot industry of the moment from cryptocurrency to Iraq dollars.

Intrepid Trader: need to make trades all the time out of a feeling of action or sense of comfort but always to the detriment of accumulating long-term gains, and more often than not, without the discipline to adjust to losses quickly. This makes one loss equal to several winners.

Nervous Nellies: watch the market too closely assuming the worst every time there's red on their screen. It's their willingness to take losses that blunt any chance at long-term investing success and making the kind of money that changes their life circumstances.

Calm Hands: usually calm, cool and collected. I prefer this profile although there are times you must have a sense of urgency.

Passive Investors

Go with the Pros: These investors usually have a long-term relationship with a broker that has crossed into a friendship. This can make it difficult for an honest critique or to take greater control. I'm not asking anyone to leave their broker, but make sure the relationship is based on outsized gains and not just having a golfing buddy.

ETFs: Passive investing is also pouring money into major ETFs (exchange traded funds) to mimic the performance of the market. This has been a disastrous approach since 2000 but more and more investors go this route, in part to save money on fees. I understand not wanting to overpay someone for mediocrity but there are better ways to put your hard-earned money to work.

401Ks and IRAs: Investors with this approach are often the most frustrated. There are several problems with this approach including limited options. If you work for a large firm that's providing matching funds, you must take advantage. But even then, you should consider controlling additional funds on your own. The passive investing craze has seen record amounts of money pour into funds that invest in exchange traded funds automatically to avoid paying a manager's fee. It works like a charm in up markets but exacerbates downside swoons.

Procrastinator

Information Collector: These would-be investors have collected so much information they could open an investment library. But the clock keeps ticking and they never get close enough to make the move and invest.

One and Done: This is someone who finally gets into the market buying one stock to "see how it goes." This approach is repeated until that one idea becomes a loser and the procrastinator goes back to the sideline.

What kind of investor are you today? To be successful in the stock market, it's important to understand how your natural instincts, your risk tolerance and previous mistakes have held back your progress.

TAKE THE BULL BY THE HORNS

Nobody cares more about your success in the stock market than you, so you should take the bull by the horns. That's the goal of this book. I'll show you how to look at the world in opportunistic ways, create a Watch List of ideas you find intriguing, then boil them down to select the best candidates for your portfolio.

The decision-making process I'll teach you is thorough and decisive, and you'll become faster with experience.

You'll make better use of your time, depending on the degree of research you're committed to doing. Each level will give you the ability to identify trading ideas or longer-term buy and hold ideas. The change in your life will shift from hours, days, weeks and even years of pondering to taking effective action.

These days, most investors are shifting toward passive investing via mutual funds and exchange traded funds that don't require any grand thinking or grand fees. Initially, these products were promoted as low-cost alternatives for investors to stretch their investing dollars. But decades of sub-par management by so-called active investors have driven buyers to look for greater returns.

As passive funds begin to control more money than active funds, risk increases. That can, and does, create a selling crisis when large positions in the fund unwind in a perpetual cycle. The more the positions move lower, the more the fund must sell, and the more the fund sells, the lower the position share prices will sink. I don't want you to be in that position.

As I mentioned above, I also consider investors that simply hand over their hard-earned money to a broker or money manager, allowing them to execute trades without questions or explanations, to be a form of passive investing. It's clear that doesn't describe anyone reading this book.

I'm even less enthralled with mutual funds.

My beef with mutual funds is that they're designed to mitigate risk and limit losses, but they also limit the ability to make money, which is your top goal. If you're a football fan, you'll understand this analogy:

In the past, the Rams were notorious for "playing not to lose" football.

Rams vs. Bills	Scoring by Quarter	
	Rams	Bills
1Q The Rams get the ball first and after two running plays throw a bomb deep down field for a touchdown. The Bills get the ball and fumble it in the shadow of their own goal. The Rams strike again with a slant pop pass over the middle. The Bills get the ball twice more in the quarter and punt both times.	14	0
2Q The Rams get the ball in great field position after the team executes a reverse on a punt, catching the Bills off guard. Two plays later the ball is softly lobbed into the corner of the endzone. The Rams miss the extra point. The teams exchange punts before the Bills finally score on a field goal. With less than a minute in the half, the Rams move the ball 80 yards on five quick pass plays before settling on a field goal before time runs out.	13	3
3Q The Bills engineer their best offensive series of the game yet settle for a chip shot field goal on the opening drive of the second half. The Rams throw another bomb taking the ball to the 12-yard line. After three running plays the team successfully kicks a field goal. Inspired by their last possession, the Bills finally put together a touchdown scoring drive.	3	13

4Q	After both teams fail to move the ball on their initial drives of the quarter, the Rams go into the "prevent" defense, which plays receivers soft allowing for short pass completions while the clock ticks down to the end of the game. The Bills take advantage and score but there are only four minutes left in the game. The coach decides to kick the ball deep and hope his defense holds. It does, and the offense gets the ball back with 53 seconds left. Two plays later, the ball is on the forty-yard line with 25 second left in the game and it looks hopeless for the Bills. But the quarterback takes the ball and, after being flushed out of the pocket with a desperate scramble, he heaves it downfield. Multiple hands go in the air but somehow a Bills receiver comes down with the ball for a touch down. The Bills go for a two-point conversion and win the game in improbable fashion.	0	15
	Final Score	30	31

The moral of the story?

In football, just as in real life, there's a vast difference between playing to win and playing not to lose. Abandoning what works, in order to run out the clock, has resulted in so many come-from-behind victories. One team starts playing to win, the other is simply trying to maintain.

This is the same with mutual funds, which often will own the hot stock in a sector but also the not-so-hot stock in a sector. If you're trying to preserve a fortune, there are other ways to do so and if you're trying to create a fortune, it's going to be virtually impossible.

I suggest that you manage a diversified portfolio. The goal will be to make the best decisions you can with the knowledge to manage both the winners and the stocks that prove to be underperformers. The ultimate goal is to create wealth and one of the necessary steps in doing that is managing risk.

You can, and should, have a diversified portfolio and still be focused on the best-value ideas with the potential to outperform projections. By the way, I also have a pet peeve about the false impression of diversification of mutual funds based on their names or stated goals.

ARE YOU DIVERSIFIED?

Let's play a game called, "Are You Diversified?" Let's assume that over the years you've bought a number of different mutual funds. You've always been careful to seek out different industries with different goals to give your portfolio balance. That's wise, but has it really worked for you?

I look at investor portfolios each week and I'm shocked at the paucity of diversification. Below is an actual review I did for a client.

They invested in five funds with great names and objectives. I looked at the top ten holdings of each and out of a possible 50 different stocks these funds only had 21 different names!

FSPTX Tech	SPYG Growth	ONEQ NASDAQ	FSTVX Performance	SWPPX S&P 500
AAPL	AAPL	AAPL	AAPL	AAPL
FB	MSFT	MSFT	MSFT	MSFT
GOOGL	FB	AMZN	AMZN	AMZN
GOOG	AMZN	FB	JNJ	JNJ
TSLA	GOOGL	GOOG	FB	FB
MSFT	GOOG	GOOGL	XOM	XOM
ADSK	JNJ	CMCSA	JPM	JPM
BABA	CMCSA	INTC	JPM	JPM
TRMB	UNH	CSCO	GOOGL	GOOGL
Global Wafer	V	AMGN	GOOG	GOOG

AAPL, FB, MSFT, GOOG and GOOGL are listed in the top ten holdings in all 5 funds.

That isn't diversification, yet the investor went to sleep each night convinced his balanced portfolio mitigated risk. By the way, when funds change their name, they generally attract 22% more new money. I find that very interesting. For the fund that new money is the real goal, after all.

I sincerely believe that in order to achieve Unstoppable Prosperity, you must control your investments individually and not through mutual funds.

THE ANALYSIS MIX: POWER OF MY THREE PILLARS

There are endless ways of analyzing individual stocks and the stock market, from quantitative to astrological. People find any number of ways to try and give themselves an edge. Over the years, the three most consistent systems of analysis have been **fundamental, technical** and **behavioral** (or sentiment). These are the Pillars of my approach to the market. An approach that has allowed me to consistently beat the market every year.

FUNDAMENTAL

Fundamental analysis allows investors to assess the future value of a company's stock based on current financial facts and trends coupled with business and economic conditions and management's ability to execute to potential and above.

All news is backward looking to a degree. Although some things lend themselves better to future assumptions than others, including industry and company trends, generally, we know when something is hot in society, from dance and song to clothes and products. But it's great to know what the numbers say and what they suggest about the future.

Part of fundamental analysis:

- Assessing financial conditions and trends
- Assessing the ability to deliver against consensus expectations
- Assessing the company's own valuations based on history and its peers
- Assessing risk

Fundamentals tell me what stocks I want to own and maintain in my portfolio.

TECHNICAL

Technical analysis allows us to understand the psyche of current shareholders and where the stock finds buyers or sellers historically. The constant gyrations of stocks are a test of shareholders who are going to feel pressure to sell every day.

Sometimes, the pressure on shareholders to close out the position and sell comes from the stock moving higher, and sometimes it's from the stock moving lower.

These shakeout periods test the resolve of shareholders.

We learn where there's *resistance* on the upside of a stock's value and where there's *support* on the downside of that value.

There are as many technical approaches to examining the market as there are stars in the sky. There was a time I used dozens of technical indicators and drove myself crazy because half would suggest selling and the other half would suggest buying.

I'll go into greater detail later in this book on the main technical indicators I employ today. The thing to remember is this: Technical analysis has nothing to do with fundamentals, with news or anything else other than patterns and history. They function as guides for when I should act.

Ultimately, I know *what* I want to own from the fundamentals and determine *when* I want to get in or out from technical signals.

BEHAVIORAL

Over time, emotions have played a larger role in short-term movement in stocks. These emotions, or sentiment, are creating a collective conventional wisdom, or conventional fear, or conventional greed, depending on circumstances.

Behaviors can be anticipated, and certainly can be leveraged, to extend gains or mitigate losses or to not take unnecessary losses. Unlike technical analysis, which is based on the learned behavior of those that own a particular asset or those that have owned it in the past, behavioral impacts the entire ecosystem around the stock including analysis and potential buyers.

For stocks, behavioral is when shares go parabolic, which means off the charts in a straight line that cannot be maintained for very long. During one of these swings, it can feel like the ultimate party or the ultimate defeat. By learning to understand and use all Three Pillars, you can ride this wave for exponential returns and you can also avoid selling into them on the downside when fear supersedes the fundamentals.

COMBINATIONS

The weighted combinations of these Three Pillars of analysis are altered depending on my objectives.

Trading

- 70% technical
- 15% fundamental
- 15% behavioral

Buying and Holding

- 70% fundamental
- 20% technical
- 10% behavioral

PILLARS OF POWER

So how has my approach performed in real life? My model portfolio has done very well. More importantly, it hasn't been a hypothetical portfolio or a social experiment where someone threw darts at a sheet of stock symbols and pretended to own those stocks, checking a year or two later and declaring they "Beat the Market."

Those kinds of experiments leave out the hardest part of investing: containing emotions and decision making that really impacts your life. I feel my job has been even more difficult because it's easier for me to take a loss with my own money than suggest to someone else such a hit is the right move.

Track records are fine but there are stocks in my model portfolio which made money, that others invested in and lost because they were too impatient to wait for alerts or second-guessed my reasoning. My goal is to empower you with the know-how and to stress the importance of discipline so that in the end you control your own destiny.

I've written this book to teach you the exact same investing approach and strategy that's allowed me to beat the market over the last 12 years - through some of the market's toughest times and some of the best of times.

I encourage you to check out my investing results at **www.unstoppableprosperity.com/paynesresults**. This page displays the results of my primary alert service for the past 12 years.

Using my Three Pillars has given me a measurable advantage in the market. Imagine how that advantage could impact your financial goals and enhance the security and comfort of your retirement.

Of course, all investments or strategies that I used to achieve these results may not be suitable for you, your particular investment objectives, financial situation or needs. I'll teach you my strategies so you can determine what is the most appropriate for you.

Throughout this chapter, we've talked about how the market works and why you need to be involved. Nothing that I've shared with you is beyond your ability to do. You can, and should, be part of the greatest wealth-producing machine the world has ever seen.

You're different from most. By reading this book you've already taken the first step to be part of this amazing opportunity. You've started on the road to Unstoppable Prosperity.

Now I want you to understand that the biggest hurdle you'll need to overcome has nothing to do with picking stocks or reading charts. No, the biggest obstacle is everyone's natural tendency towards inaction. That's something that we have to resist. You've taken a HUGE first step with this book, but the seduction of inaction is really strong. There may be times you want to "do it later" or "think about it a while longer." Almost always, when you put it off, you put it away.

As you go through this book, I've provided action items for you at the end of each chapter. Do these. They provide the practice that will help you build the confidence to act. I know that everyone can be hesitant when it comes to making decisions that involve money, I get that. But I also know that the sooner you trust your knowledge, and the lessons you'll learn through this book, the sooner you'll be on the road to Unstoppable Prosperity.

CHAPTER TWO

BUILDING A WATCH LIST PHASE 1:
QUICK FUNDAMENTAL ANALYSIS

One of my goals is to empower you to make money on what you already know but never had the confidence or ability to leverage into an investment plan. For example, my mom helped me make a lot of money for myself and for other people, by turning me on to Burlington Coat Factory and TJ Maxx.

When my mom would come to visit us, I would take parts of the weekend to spend time with her. Invariably, we always went to her favorite stores. In fact, we'd spend a couple of hours in each store. I'd find some place to sit and watch her and all the other shoppers, patiently combing aisle after aisle looking for the perfect item at the perfect price.

For certain shoppers, this was nirvana - the ultimate retail bargain hunting experience that couldn't be duplicated on the internet or department stores. After one of those long shopping days, I went home and began to research the fundamentals of Burlington Coat Factory. I liked what I saw and put the stock on my potential Buy List.

My son has also been a valuable source of information. He's given me a heads up on trends and timing for companies like Hasbro and Urban Outfitters. My wife saved me a lot of money by pointing out why she avoided certain stores and products. Every single time she was right as bad news would eventually come out and shares of those companies took big hits.

Even at work I take notice of trends and what people are talking about, especially on the elevator. For instance, I saw the Marc Jacobs "big watch" craze while riding the elevators at work. I saw all the young ladies begin to buy gold watches with large bezels - once considered too large for women's wrists.

I'm not a very hip guy so it's important that I observe the world around me, paying attention to nuanced changes, watching to catch the wave of something new and exciting. I've become very adept at seeing changes. But I must admit, I also ask people around me, especially younger members of my family and employees, about what's new on the scene and what's catching everyone's attention where they hang out.

Of course, nowadays we're greeted online with clickbait, gossip and articles on what's cool and hip and what the future will look like from a variety of sources. Unfortunately for most people, connecting the dots to make money on these burgeoning trends never starts.

Ironically, the same people that want to be first to spend their money on being in the hip crowd never consider owning the companies that produce the items they're willing to stand in line to buy. Those people would be the first to tell me they don't know anything about the stock market. I get it. This wasn't taught in schools and if your parents weren't in the market it seems foreign and forbidding.

In fact, keeping the stock market mysterious is how Wall Street gets to make money when most folks finally decide to give it a try.

This notion of buying, or at least leveraging, what you know was made popular by money manager Peter Lynch. He famously said, "Invest in what you know." This message was heard by many already in the stock market but was never a clarion call to the masses that simply never thought about it because it seemed so far out of their reach. Sure, there's more than just investing in what you know. What you're familiar with is a great place to begin but from there it takes some work.

The idea of researching something, even if you feel you know the product or the service well, is important to understanding the "fundamentals." I've seen doctors lose tons of money on drug stocks because they fall in love with the story and feel they "knew" it was going to be a winner even as the companies that produce the drug continued to come up short. I've seen the same mistake made by engineers when it comes to technology stocks. If you become so emotionally invested in a product, based solely on your personal or professional experience, it becomes difficult to see when the company behind the product may be a poor investment.

Moreover, when you become too much of a fan, even knowing there are issues with the company or product living up to the hype, you'll continue to hold onto the stock. Investing is different than rooting for the hometown team. The key to this book is to allow you to pursue investment winners and come to grips with losers or ideas that stop working.

Of course, there are going to be times when you sour on a product or company you were head over heels in love with at one point for a variety of reasons. Make sure you use that new information in addressing your portfolio. Using the information you gather from family and friends cannot only tell you when to buy a stock but can also give you information that may cause you to sell. Let me give you an example.

I was visiting with some friends when their 25-year-old son told me that SnapChat had made changes to their platform and he thought those changes were disastrous. I didn't understand what he was saying about the feature, but I understood his passion as a (formerly) dedicated user.

The stock was trading around $13.00 a share when he predicted this move to be a disaster. Three days later, a couple of superstars in the world of entertainment and millennial influence made the same observation. The stock collapsed. Six months later, the shares were changing hands down more than 50%.

So, make no mistake, you already possess a wealth of great investment ideas that just need to be tapped through your own experiences and expertise. You also have access to a much broader base of knowledge if you observe the world around you and talk to friends and family about what's new and exciting (or changing, in the case of SnapChat) in their world.

PAYING ATTENTION AND PREPARING FOR THE WORLD TO COME

Every investor must have and maintain a list of stocks that could be potential candidates to add to their portfolio.

In addition to paying attention to things in your everyday life, investors need to be aware of societal trends and events. We all know about how the internet will connect our refrigerator to the supermarket and how drones will bring milk and eggs to our front door because the system knows we've run out.

That future is going to see amazing things, once only thought to be science fiction, come to fruition. The future is rushing at us faster and faster each day. It's easy to assume each new product or idea or service is ready to explode and become that grand slam "next big thing" we're all looking for. However, sometimes the "next big thing" is just a bit ahead of its time. By the same token, sometimes the stuff of dreams and imagination come true but just don't have the impact we assumed.

And then there are times when something sounds great, is unveiled and falls flat, only to hang around and eventually live up to the hype. I've seen this so many times - especially in technology. That's why we build a Watch List, to be ready to move if we find that grand slam but also to give us a chance to let our emotions cool and make sure that the stock we want is on a solid footing. We'll look at technicals in the next chapter which will help us determine if this is the right time to buy as well.

Let me give you an example of what I mean by looking at a product that was ahead of its time but eventually fulfilled its promise.

3D PRINTING IS THE FUTURE!?!

I believe I was the first person to discuss and recommend 3D printing stocks on TV and I was trying to position investors even before then. My experience demonstrates each scenario that comes with getting in front of hot trends.

My favorite name in the 3D printing industry is Stratasys (SSYS), which I've recommended many times over the years.

- **Too Soon** - I thought Stratasys was a buy on July 18, 2003 but the stock essentially moved sideways for years.
- **Perfect Timing** - The next time I recommended the

stock was August 29, 2012. By the end of 2013 the
stock was up 100%.

- **A Dud** - From that peak at the end of December 2013 to
  February 2016 the stock lost 90% of its value after missing
  financial assumptions and losing business traction.

The 3D industry has lost that "wow factor" but I'm sure
there'll be another time to own these companies since the
technology will eventually build everything from factories to
houses to complicated machinery.

The point of this example is to show how "hot stocks" can
appear to be "can't miss" opportunities and may even soar
for some period of time. But, sometimes, the consuming
public isn't ready for them. In the case of Stratasys, investors
and consumers basically ignored the stock for several years.
Then, in the last part of 2012 and through 2013 the stock
shot up like a rocket (we'll look at reasons for these types
of increases later in the book). But the increase couldn't
be sustained. The fundamentals that had caused the stock
to move sideways for years were still the same when the
increase occurred, making that increase unsustainable and
resulting in the major pullback.

Investing Lesson

Everyone loves an exciting story and things that thrill
the imagination. Wall Street is no exception where they
see hundred-dollar bills coming out the exhaust pipes of
flying cars. I'm not suggesting you shouldn't be excited
about new things and "out of the box" ideas. You should
absolutely have those kinds of names on your potential
investment Buy List. You just must understand how they
normally perform in real life. You have to have realistic
expectations and you must do the appropriate research (I'll
show you how in just a bit).

There were once hundreds of car companies that got whittled down to three and hundreds of railroads that got whittled down to five. There were thousands of computer hardware and software companies when the tech bubble popped. Every period of paradigm change in industry has brought about paradigm changes in investing.

My goal for you isn't to be bemused or whine about market circumstance. My investing principles are mostly along the lines of old school research that also acknowledges modern day influences. I find all the machine trading and rules-stripping to help intuitions worrisome and unfair, but the goal in investing and in this book remains the same. Understand the stock market and what makes it tick, both near-term and long-term, to fulfill the goal of you attaining Unstoppable Prosperity.

POSITIONING FOR NEAR-TERM POPS

This is such an exciting time. There's so much great stuff ready to make the leap off drawing boards and into our lives. These new ideas will generate untold fortunes.

This will happen in technology; this will happen with cannabis; and with every other major wave that will change our lives over time. But what's going to change our lives in the next six months? That's the question smart investors need to be asking themselves. So, what do you need to be looking at to determine what stocks to put on your Watch List? My Watch List is made up of stocks that I think are worth exploring. These are the stocks that I'm going to research to determine if the fundamentals of the company justify investing in them. I've already explained how I use friends and family, along with my own observations, to identify companies of interest. Let me give you an example that came right out of national headlines not too long ago.

Back in the summer of 2016, America was in the midst of the most fantastic election in a generation. No matter what side of the political aisle an individual might be on, the battle between Donald Trump and Hillary Clinton was one for the ages. While all the attention was on debates, news bombshells, and where the latest poll numbers were, what remained unseen by many was that the U.S. economy was finally firming up in anticipation of new blood in the White House.

Corporate earnings calls talked more about investments and lots of data points improved. I was thinking about what companies would win based on the two possible outcomes. My focus shifted to potential investment winners no matter which candidate would become Commander in Chief. My investment thesis looked at business relief, unleashing of pent-up optimism and business investment.

I've always said that when measuring the impact of a presidential term on the stock market, it's smart, fair and honest to begin the day after the election because that's when big money begins to make its move. At that very moment businesses, both large and small, have an idea of changes in laws, regulations and taxes that are coming, and they don't wait. This is also true for large investors, and, of course, true for small investors looking to make money.

Remember, when you're putting together and monitoring your Watch List it begins with the things that impact your life but goes beyond just stuff and people you like. Sure, if you don't like weapons you can skip defense contractor stocks but be careful not to let your political ideology or personal preference limit your opportunities to improve your own economic circumstances and change your own family's lives.

Hillary Clinton had enough Wall Street donors to make me think she would halt the anti-business environment, especially those draconian actions that crushed manufacturing along with oil and gas production. I was sure a President Trump would go even further in unwinding those actions. This was important to me because unleashing business investment was a critical component to returning the United States to 3% annual growth or more, which some had come to believe could never be done again. So, it appeared to me that either candidate was going to be good for businesses, and, by extension, good for the market. The next step was to determine if there was an area of common ground where I felt both candidates would be willing to push forward.

The wheels didn't have to turn much to find the economic issue both candidates agreed upon: Infrastructure Spending.

For me this was low-hanging fruit and an easy sell for both parties in a nation where everyone worried about crumbling roads and falling bridges. When was the last time anyone ran for President of the United States and didn't deride the nation's "crumbling roads and bridges?" The fact is, every politician in every country talks of infrastructure building and many follow through even though the long-term wisdom is questionable. From ghost cities in China and empty, never-used airports in Spain, the money spent was to calm public outrage and manufacture instant job creation.

And our two candidates for the White House played their own version of the game, "I Can Top That." Each week saw them leapfrogging one another with the amount of money they would use to make sure the roads were safe enough for the family to visit grandma.

Hillary Clinton

- $275 billion, five-year plan to rebuild our infrastructure
- Repair and expand our roads and bridges
- Lower transportation costs and unlock economic

opportunity by expanding public transit options

- Connect all Americans to the internet
- Invest in building world-class American airports and modernize our national airspace system

Donald Trump

- $1 trillion on a variety of infrastructure projects over 10 years
- Tax credits to private companies to finance projects
- $167 billion equity investment
- Debt limited through the use of private partnerships

All of this information was out there for everyone to see. I just chose to look at it through the lens of an investor, which is what I want you to do as well. To add to the political rhetoric, there was a sense of urgency as Americans were aware of horrible conditions and mounting costs to make repairs. From 2009 to 2013, the cost swelled from $2.2 trillion to $3.6 trillion as conditions continued to deteriorate. A quick search provided me with this information:

CATEGORY	1988*	1998	2001	2005	2009	2013
Aviation	B-	C-	D	D+	D	D
Bridges	–	C-	C	C	C	C+
Dams	–	D	D	D+	D	D
Drinking Water	B-	D	D	D-	D-	D
Energy	–	–	D+	D	D+	D+
Hazardous Waste	D	D-	D+	D	D	D
Inland Waterways	B-	–	D+	D-	D-	D-
Levees	–	–	–	–	D-	D-
Rail	–	–	–	C-	C-	C+
Roads	C+	D-	D+	D	D-	D

Schools	D	F	D-	D	D	D
Solid Waste	C-	C-	C+	C+	C+	B-
Transit	C-	C-	C-	D+	D	D
Wastewater	C	D+	D	D-	D-	D
GPA	C	D	D+	D	D	D+
Cost to Improve**	-	-	$1.3T	$1.6T	$2.2T	$3.6T

Source: American Society of Civil Engineers (ASCE) Report Card
https://www.infrastructurereportcard.org/

Despite these numbers, I considered the impact on the Federal Deficit as a possible limiting factor. Again, a little quick research provided me some interesting information.

Despite a massive federal deficit, public spending as a percentage of government spending reached a plateau in 2001 then drifted from there. This was another fact that would give either candidate political cover to push for something massive once in office.

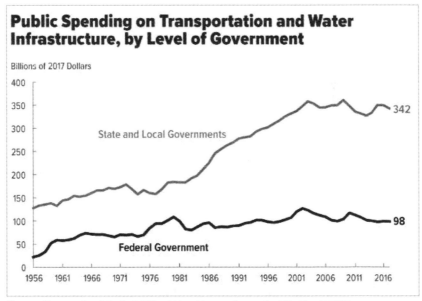

Public Spending on Transportation and Water Infrastructure, by Level of Government

Source: Congressional Budget Office https://www.cbo.gov/publication/54539

MY INFRASTRUCTURE WATCH LIST

As someone that's not in the infrastructure business, I immediately began thinking about machinery I see at construction sites. Names that came immediately to mind included:

Caterpillar (CAT)

John Deere (DE)

Illinois Tool Works (ITW)

United Rentals (URI)

This would've made a very usable Watch List, but that was just my preliminary list. I knew I needed to drill deeper, so I researched more and learned there were many other nuances to the kind of business opportunities for a national infrastructure program. I eventually narrowed it down to a few engineering companies and these became the focus of my Watch List:

MasTec (MTZ)

Quanta Services (PWR)

EMCOR Group (EME)

Granite Construction (GVA)

By late November, the outcome of the Presidential election was known and immediately things began to change in the stock market and in the business world. There was a sense of urgency to get long (buy) stocks for short-term gains but also as investments on a Trump Presidency.

With that in mind, I began refining my Watch List. I began doing some basic research into the companies I had identified as possibilities. I'm going to walk you through that process now. It's important that you follow and understand each of these steps.

KNOW THE PEOPLE

As you build and maintain your Watch List, I encourage everyone to learn as much about a company's history as possible. This often sets the business ethos that will also make you more comfortable as an investor. When I investigated MasTec (MTZ), I came across the quintessential American story.

It was started by two unemployed carpenters in the same year as the great stock market crash and beginning of the Great Depression, 1929. The company made huge strides and became a global name in the industry by the time management turned to a Cuban immigrant to lead it to greater glory.

I loved the story and felt I understood the current management team, who are the progeny of that Cuban immigrant and committed to the excellence he brought. As an investor, you should know about the executive team that you're considering hiring, as a shareholder, to operate the business and be stewards of your money.

Like hot new ideas, inspiring stories don't always lead to good investments. Knowing the people is an important first step, no doubt about that, but it's only the first step.

QUICK LOOK RESEARCH TO MAKE REAL-TIME INVESTMENTS

After reviewing the potentially biggest winners for a major infrastructure investment, I needed to monitor them further fundamentally and technically. These analytical approaches can be varied and endless, but I've developed a *quick look methodology* that really works. While this book will later show you more complex approaches to both forms of analysis, these are ways to leverage expertise that actually allows you to beat the experts.

There are so many layers of investing theories and approaches one could spend a lifetime learning them and I have. While each arms you with more knowledge, the fact is they begin to counteract each other and can lead to confusion. Just like so many other things in life that can be explained in a stack of manuals but in real application require much less information, you can make big money in the stock market using my quick research techniques.

I'll share those with you and I'll also share methods I employ to dive deeper and learn more. But I'm not going to inundate you in investment theory and approaches that would only intimidate and confuse you.

QUICK FUNDAMENTAL SEARCH

Fundamental analysis is the backbone of successful investing. It gives you knowledge, which is the ultimate source of empowerment, allowing you to buy or sell stocks based on factual developments, trends and valuations rather than widespread hysteria or our own self-destructive habits.

The main goal of fundamental analysis is to determine intrinsic value in a company. There are several ways to measure and determine value. We need to dive deeper and deeper, crunch data and form intelligent assumptions supported by factual inputs.

The fastest way to understand and determine the state of any publicly traded company is to check the earnings history and trends. It's not unlike saying the best way to assess the best team is to look at the score after the game. Sure, there can be upsets, but often the best team wins and there are signs during the game about the outcome.

Let's face it, the bottom line is the bottom line and earnings are the bottom line in the stock market.

Looking at historic earnings performance and trends is a crucial first step. It becomes even more powerful when coupled with future earnings assumptions being done by professional analysts. These professionals make their living speaking to companies, listening to conference calls, checking with suppliers and evaluating all aspects of a business. Using the information from these professionals is an easy and effective way for you to assess publicly traded company fundamentals.

In effect, you put all of the Wall Street analysts to work for you to act as your guide in making investment decisions or to augment work you do independently.

I stress my *quick analysis approach*, which focuses on finding the best ideas to consider buying. I then couple the fundamental review with a quick technical view. This helps us determine when to act on the ideas at the top of our Watch List. Essentially, **fundamentals tell us *what* to buy while technicals tell us *when* to buy**. When creating our Watch List, we want to do a quick check on the most important fundamentals and technicals to determine if the company warrants a deeper dive (which we'll talk about in Chapters 8 and 9).

With that overview, let's take a step back and look at what I consider are the two most crucial elements of my quick look fundamental analysis.

#1 - HISTORIC EARNINGS RESULTS

Using the Watch List I assembled on the eve of the 2016 Presidential campaign, I began to monitor all the names on that list for changes in earnings estimates, share activity and price.

There are free and inexpensive services online to help you catch up on the earnings history and market reaction. Here are a few to check out:

Yahoo Finance - finance.yahoo.com

NASDAQ - nasdaq.com

Google Finance - google.com/finance

Financial Visualizations - finviz.com

Major Wall Street firms have armies of analysts and investment professionals and have access to the upper echelons of companies that trade in the public market. These analysts meet and get to question businesses and evaluate the ecosphere of suppliers and customers. This insight is valuable for many reasons. You should be aware of what these analysts are learning. It's the collective opinions of these analysts that will forge a consensus that essentially establishes expectations and becomes the ultimate grading mechanism for a publicly traded company.

Publicly traded company management plays a vital role in establishing consensus since it's their own guidance that's often the basis for Wall Street expectations.

For this reason, earnings and guidance trigger the biggest moves in stock prices, sometimes resulting in overreactions. Your goal is to assess the fundamental valuation proposition and make the appropriate decisions about your investment.

History of Execution

For **buy and hold** investments, I've always preferred buying stocks that've gone at least one-year reporting financial results, especially earnings, that've beaten the Street. The ability to "beat the Street" underscores the management's ability to execute and corroborates the viability of the investment thesis.

It's true there are lots of ways for management to find shortcuts for beating the street, which is why there are deeper levels of fundamental research one can and should do. But one quick and very reliable source for the quality of earnings results is the reaction of the stock. Is it going up in price or not? Is this "good news" in the earnings report and the stock beating expectations viewed as reliable or not? The stock will give you a good indication.

Momentum of Earnings

In addition to consistently beating Wall Street expectations, I hold more credence in companies that have a string of earnings that beat the Street by a greater and greater margin. That means in each successive quarter, not only are results better than Wall Street consensus, but better by wider margins than the prior quarter and year ago comparable period.

This suggests a company is performing so well that Wall Street can't keep up with its progress (and neither has the underlying share price).

MasTec (MTZ) saw its financial fortunes reverse and, along the way, the share price began to reflect this as well. After four straight quarters of earnings that beat the Street and strong momentum higher, the stock passed the initial phase of the quick fundamental test.

MTZ EARNINGS RESULTS AND WALL STREET REACTION				
DATE	CONSENSUS	ACTUAL	DIFFERENCE	SHARE PRICE REACTION 1 WEEK LATER
NOV 3, 2016	$0.69	$0.81	+$0.12	+17.8%
AUG 4, 2016	$0.23	$0.36	+$0.13	+22.9%
MAY 5, 2016	-$0.02	$0.02	+$0.04	-1.2%
FEB 25, 2016	$0.12	$0.21	+$0.09	+26.9%
NOV 3, 2015	$0.33	$0.26	-$0.07	+0.7%
AUG 17, 2015	$0.15	$0.10	-$0.05	-13.8%
MAY 11, 2015	$0.18	$0.07	-$0.11	-6.4%
FEB 26, 2015	$0.38	$0.40	+0.02	-0.0%

Look at the trend and you can see where momentum was building, and the stock was becoming a screaming buy.

The MTZ third quarter of 2016 ended on September 30th, 2016 and the company crunched all the numbers and released those financial results on November 3, 2016. The company posted earnings per share of $0.81. The Street was expecting $0.69 which means the actual results came in $0.12 ahead of consensus or 17.4% better.

The earnings beat was substantially larger than the prior quarter and a year earlier, which are clear buy signals.

The stock looked attractive because nothing drives share price like margins expanding and earnings growing and coming in better than the Wall Street consensus estimate. This is an investable trend.

Shares of MTZ were changing hands at $28.30 at the close of trading on the afternoon management released financial results. One week later on November 10, 2016 the shares closed at $33.35. The reaction was a 17.8% increase in share value.

#2 - FUTURE EARNINGS TRENDS

Once we see management not only beating the Street but posting results that come in even stronger in the most recent quarters, we look to the future. I'm looking for future earnings consensus. Changes in earnings estimates, either higher or lower, point to Wall Street's acknowledgement that fundamentals are improving or deteriorating.

This is one of my favorite quick assessment tools and it's extremely effective. This works for two reasons:

1. Even as earnings are being adjusted, Wall Street usually still underestimates actual results.

2. The herd mentality means that after one analyst adjusts his numbers others are going to follow.

Since our goal is long-term prosperity, my focus is on a longer-term investment so I check out trends for earnings in the next fiscal year.

On November 28, 2016, MTZ's 'Next Year' earnings consensus spiked to $2.08 from $1.96 (see chart below), dovetailing strongly with the trend over the past 52 weeks. This was the second phase of my quick fundamental research process and a clear BUY SIGNAL.

By the way, that quarter's earnings consensus edged higher on the eve of the release, again suggesting Wall Street analysts were being caught flat-footed and were trying to catch up.

EPS TREND	CURRENT QTR.	NEXT QTR.	CURRENT YEAR	NEXT YEAR
CURRENT ESTIMATE	0.54	0.23	1.74	2.08
7 DAYS AGO	0.53	0.24	1.74	2.08
30 DAYS AGO	0.51	0.24	1.58	1.96
60 DAYS AGO	0.51	0.24	1.58	1.96
90 DAYS AGO	0.51	0.24	1.58	1.97

BUILDING THE CASE TO GO FROM WATCH LIST TO BUY LIST

MTZ's actual earnings turned around and gained momentum with successive quarters more impressive than the last quarter. This kind of earnings momentum has to play a major role in your decision making.

When businesses turn around and begin to execute, there's normally a lot of room in the stock to make an investment since it'll take a fair amount of time before Wall Street jumps completely on board.

On that note, I began to see sharp increases in earnings consensus, which had to be driven by a realization by those that followed the stock that the fundamentals were improving.

Fundamental analysis plays the greatest role in my personal decision-making process once I know what I want to buy long term. But for shorter-term potential buys, technical analysis (charts and volume) can make you a lot of money. The financial media has established a rivalry between technical and fundamental analysis, but I believe individual investors should incorporate both.

NOW YOU KNOW

Now that you've completed the quick fundamental analysis, the next step is to make sure we have a corroborating technical buy signal – in fact, with all the other factors moving quickly it's important to seek and identify that buy signal quickly as well.

I want to emphasize here that in most cases you'll want to do more fundamental analysis before making a buy. I go into more detail about how to do that in Chapter 8, Fundamentals - A Deeper Dive. On occasion you may come across a potential buy that seems so strong you want to act more quickly. When that rare opportunity presents itself, I want you to be prepared to act. In order to do that, you need to have a basic understanding of how technicals can provide guidance. The next chapter gives you an introduction of how I use technicals in my investing approach.

NOW EXECUTE

In this chapter I've given you the most important fundamental factors to look at when evaluating an investment opportunity. Now it's time to apply that knowledge. Because there's so much here, don't hesitate to refer back to each step along the way.

Pick a few stocks from the world around you, something you're interested in and would be willing to learn more about. Look at any information you can find about the company and its management team, watching specifically for anything that might be a really positive sign or possibly a red flag.

Look at the bottom line for the company. Is it strong? Can you determine whether the current management team is making good decisions and maximizing the potential of the company?

Next, look at what Wall Street is projecting for the company. Has the company exceeded past expectations?

Ultimately, there are two main factors that are most important in my quick fundamental analysis:

1. Historic Earnings Results
2. Future Earnings Trends

If you find that the fundamentals are not positive, for whatever reason, select another company and repeat the process before moving on. After all, knowing *what* to buy is the most important first step! Practice, Practice, Practice!

Practicing this "quick look" fundamental analysis will help you know which stocks should be placed on your Watch List. We'll dive deeper into fundamental analysis in Chapter 8 to determine if they should stay there.

CHAPTER THREE

BUILDING A WATCH LIST PHASE 2:
QUICK TECHNICAL ANALYSIS

Like fundamentals, I'll give you a more in-depth look at technicals later in the book in Chapter 9. However, I want you to have an understanding of this basic analysis so that you're prepared to act if that "unicorn" appears and you want to act quickly.

Technical analysis is another way of saying that we're going to look at stock charts. If you're new to investing, and even if you aren't, charts can be intimidating. That's something I'll help you get over. Charts are an important tool with respect to sustainable wealth building and one that you must use.

Let me briefly describe what a chart is and then explain why they're important.

A stock's chart shows us past price and volume histories over a certain period of time. Simply put, charts help us look at trends in the price and volume of a given stock. Is the price going up or down? Is the stock trading on greater or lesser volume than in the past? This information is used by both traders and investors to anticipate what the stock is likely going to do in the near future.

Analysts who study charts have identified recurring patterns, known as formations, that often precede turning points in stock prices. They've also developed tools to use when tracking stocks to spot unusual activity. Unusual activity can be another way to tip us off to explosive potential movement in the near future.

Naturally, with so much at stake, chartists have developed a number of methods and approaches when it comes to forecasting stock movement based upon price histories. I'll cover a few of my favorite chart formations and what they mean in this chapter and go into more details on top technical indicators I prefer to use later in Chapter 9. For now, it's enough to understand that charts provide value, historic and predictive information about a stock we've researched and are interested in buying.

We need to use these "technicals" to pinpoint the best times to either buy or sell a stock. Effectively using technicals can help us anticipate when a stock is getting ready to move in either direction. Picking the best time to buy, or avoiding a poor time to buy, can make a significant difference in the profit you realize from any given position.

At the same time, using charts can help us recognize a downturn before it becomes a panic and we're caught with a stock that has become a real loser.

Whether you're focused on short-term trading or long-term investing, understanding how to read charts will make an enormous difference to your results. While charts are an important tool, they should never become an excuse for not acting!

At first glance, the number of technical tools available can be overwhelming. But that's just a first impression. The truth is that you don't need all of them. Learning a few charting tools and patterns will provide solid information from which to make a decision.

I've provided a list of charting techniques and indicators on the next page that you might find listed by various professionals. "Techniques" can be thought of as a method a chartist applies to the charting data.

An "indicator" is normally some sort of mathematical computation based on prior price and volume action that helps to illuminate something our naked eyes tend to overlook. Keep in mind, though over 100 tools are listed, this is but a mere start! There are thousands at this point! Which is why I'm going to give you several that I like and explain how I use them. In the meantime, we'll focus on a quick way to use charts so that we find good buying or selling opportunities to use in our own portfolios.

Yahoo! Finance offers all these indicators on their free charting system:		
1. Moving Average	41. Elder Impulse System	81. Prime Number Oscillators
2. Moving Average Envelope	42. Elder Ray Index	82. Pring's Know Sure Thing
3. Moving Average Deviation	43. Franctal Chaos Bands	83. Pring's Special K
4. Collinger Bands	44. Fractal Chaos Oscillator	84. Psychological Line
5. RSI	45. Gator Oscillator	85. QStick
6. MACD	46. Gopalakrishnan Range Index	86. Rainbow Moving Average
7. All Indicators	47. High Low Bands	87. Rainbow Oscillator
8. Accumulation / Distribution	48. High Minus Low	89. RAVI
9. Accumulative Swing Index	49. Highest High Value	90. Relative Vigor Index
10. ADX / DMS	50. Historical Volatility	91. Relative Volatility
11. Alligator	51. Ichimoku Clouds	92. RSI
12. Anchored VWAP	52. Intraday Momentum Index	93. Schaff Trend Cycle
13. Aroon	53. Keltner Channel	94. Shinchara Intensity Ratio
14. Aroon Oscillator	54. Klinger Volume Oscillator	94. Shinchara Intensity Ratio
15. ATR Bands	55. Linear Reg Forcast	95. Standard Deviation
16. ATR Training Stops	56. Linear Reg Intercept	96. STARC Bands
17. Average True Range	57. Linear Reg R2	97. Stochastic Momentum Index
18. Awesome Oscillator	58. Linear Reg Slope	98. Stochastics
19. Balance of Power	59. Lowest Low Value	99. Supertrend
20. Beta	60. MACD	100. Swing Index
21. Bollinger %b	61. Market Facilitation Index	101. Time Series Forecast
22. Bollinger Bands	62. Mass Index	102. Trade Volume Index
23. Bollinger Bandwidth	63. Median Price	103. Trend Intesity Index
24. Center of Gravity	64. Momentum Indicator	104. TRIX
25. Chaikin Money Flow	65. Money Flow Index	105. True Range
26. Chaikin Volatility	66. Moving Average	106. Twiggs Money Flow
27. Chande Forecast Oscillator	67. Moving Average Deviation	107. Typical Price
28. Chande Momentum Oscillator	68. Moving Average Envelope	108. Ulcer Index
29. Choppiness Index	69. Negative Volume Index	109. Ultimate Oscillator
30. Commodity Channel Index	70. On Balance Volume	110. Valuation Lines
31. Coppock Curve	71. Parabolic SAR	111. Vertical Horizontal Filter
32. Correlation Coefficient	72. Performance Index	112. Volume Chart
33. Darvas Box	73. Pivot Points	113. Volume Oscillator
34. Detrended Price Oscillator	74. Positive Volume Index	114. Volume Profile
35. Disparity Index	75. Pretty Good Oscillator	115. Volume Rate of Change
36. Donchian Channel	76. Price Momentum Oscillator	116. Vortex Indicator
37. Donchian Width	77. Price Oscillator	117. WWAP
38. Ease of Movement	78. Price Rate of Change	118. Weighted Close
39. Ehler Fisher Transform	79. Price Volume Trend	119. Williams %R
40. Elder Force Index	80. Prime Number Bands	120. ZigZag

If you watch financial television or read financial publications, you might think that you'd either use fundamental analysis or technical analysis to make decisions about investing. As I mentioned previously, there seems to be a contrived rivalry in the media about this. I think that's foolish. You should use *both* and gather as much information as possible to maximize your preparedness before initiating a position in a stock.

UNDERSTANDING CHART FORMATIONS

I'll share more detailed technical information in Chapter 9, but for now you can do what I do most of the time and simply eyeball the chart to spot a buy signal. When it comes to charting, I try to keep it simple, especially in the early stages of analyzing a stock.

The key with charts is to measure risk and reward adjusted for the factor of time or timing. When I know what stocks I want to own, all I need is to know *when* to buy them. This is where charts come in since, to me, they provide the key to action. There are many potential "buy signals" from charts and the action in stock prices.

SUPPORT AND RESISTANCE

Before we start to move along too fast and get ahead of ourselves, we need to briefly cover support and resistance. There may not be anything more fundamental and important when it comes to technical analysis.

First up, **support**. Note in the S&P Homebuilders ETF (XHB) chart below that the stock price touched very close to $38.49 before eventually giving way. Chartists would have labeled that a "support level" due to the number of times the stock price respected that area and "bounced" back up after "touching" it.

Resistance is the counterpart to support. Notice how many times Verizon's (VZ) stock price struggled to push above $55.40 before it was finally able to surmount that level in late October. It respected that level several times, there's no doubt about that.

Support and Resistance reflect the value that the market currently places on the stock. Investors aren't willing to pay more than a certain amount for a stock and view it as a good "bargain" when it nears the "support" levels. These two concepts are very important to understand.

Above in the S&P Biotech ETF (XBI) chart we see a rectangle pattern which is also referred to as a flat channel by some.

The stock price remains range-bound between the $92.50 support level and the $101.25 resistance level for several months. In late September, a rally attempt fails to elevate the stock back up towards the top of the rectangle and stalls out before reaching $100.00 at #1. The stock price weakens from there and closes below the mid-September low near $94.00 but above the $92.50 support level. This is the first tip off that there could be a serious technical issue developing. Once the stock price weakens further and closes below $92.50 support, a technical breakdown ensues and the price begins to cascade lower at #2. To be clear, the stock could have broken out towards the upside had it decisively breached the $101.25 resistance level. However, the entire stock market came under heavy selling pressure in the fall of 2018 and that overall weakness contributed to XBI's decline.

Support and resistance lines can be drawn on an angle as well. If a stock's price is trending and it keeps respecting lows and highs that we can connect with an angled line, a channel can often be seen:

CenturyLink Inc.'s (CTL) stock was already under selling pressure starting in late August 2018. It began to make a series of lower highs and lower lows for several more months as it traced out an angular channel formation. Unfortunately, matters only worsened for CTL in mid-November when the channel's support line began to fail. The stock price made one last ditch effort to reclaim the channel in early December. That attempt promptly failed and channel support was breached decisively. That ushered in cascade-style selling which rapidly brought prices much lower.

This channel indicates a trend for the stock and needs our attention. In the chart above we might not want to invest in the stock at this time, based on the direction of the channel.

When thinking about resistance and support, think upside and downside price levels where stocks stop and turn the other way. These points are usually fairly-stout and hold through several attempts to pierce them and, in the process, they become important technical points as time marches on.

Here are two critical points to remember:

Former resistance often becomes support. When a stock is able to finally go above a resistance level and remain there for a period of time, we know that investors have determined that the value of the stock has increased for some reason.

Former support often becomes resistance. Likewise, when a stock falls below a support level and remains there, the support level often becomes the new resistance level. This also indicates that investors have determined a new (lower) value for that stock.

This fact is critical to remember as it will be a useful guide when looking for entry and exit points. In fact, these lines can remain influential for traders and investors years later.

Here's an example of resistance becoming support and sequentially a "buy signal":

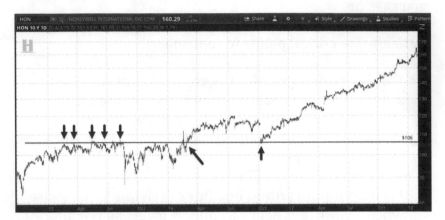

From 2015 through early 2016, shares of Honeywell (HON) repeatedly saw rallies stall around $106 and turn lower. This action is known as "backing and filling" since repeated efforts to break resistance always led to a sizable pullback.

After a year of attempts to clear that resistance (see down arrows), shares of Honeywell finally broke out in March 2016 closing above $106.00. The stock went on to rally 13% to a high of $113.83 by July before pulling back. By early October, the stock stumbled back to that former resistance point which then acted as support.

The stock holding at support, which was once resistance, became a major buy signal (see up arrow).

BREAKOUTS

There are several ways to establish resistance points in a stock price or indices or other investment instruments and to watch for a move past one of these formidable barriers. Again, resistance points, which are also known as levels, are those prices that a stock seems unable to go above and remain for any length of time.

These resistance points represent the points where sellers have overwhelmed buyers and driven the stock lower. When a stock does break through one of these levels, it's known as a "breakout" and it's the exact moment you should consider buying the stock, assuming you've done your due diligence and know you want to own it.

Lumentum Holdings Inc.'s (LITE) chart demonstrates a breakout very well. It's stock price struggled many times near the $54.10 resistance level. Finally, in early February, the stock was able to decisively push through that level and performed very well for some time afterward.

My goal in emphasizing breakouts is to help you stop all the excuses and rationale for not buying and to take action when you see these amazing opportunities.

Let's have a look at another instance wherein MasTec Inc. (MTZ) broke out. This type of action happens repeatedly in the markets and I want you to believe in it by seeing it. Notice that MTZ respected the $31.29 level as it was fighting its way back up from the $12.44 low that was made in early 2016. After trying and then pulling back a little at that level, it finally pushed through very strongly.

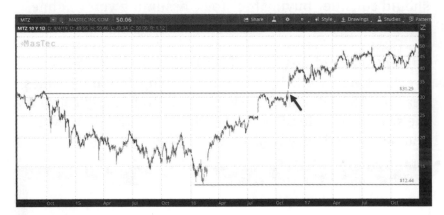

Another aspect that I'd like to introduce is trading volume. In the MTZ chart below, a volume subgraph has been added so that we can monitor how many shares of stock correspond to the price action we see in the price graph. With this additional information, we can see that the trading volume was also moving up at the same time. Those two events together are a very good sign!

When a breakout occurs, some technicians (folks that invest primarily by using charts) like to see (upside) resistance broken and then be "tested" at least once. This would indicate that the resistance level is now the support level. VZ's graph below is a fine example of this type of behavior.

Please note how VZ struggled mightily to surpass $55.40 for about 3 months. In late October it blasted up past that level but then pulled back to it not once but twice. In doing this, VZ is thought to have *converted* what was resistance into support. From there it was able to launch a sustained rally, which, is exactly what we're after!

I think about buying breakouts like the Medulla Oblongata part of our brain which governs automatic functions like breathing and heart rate. We consider these functions to be instinctive, but we think about them in ways that we don't have to "think" about them. Buying breakouts should become that kind of an instinctive action when coupled with proper fundamental knowledge. This is true for trades and for establishing long-term investments.

Moreover, depending on overall market conditions, charts can inform us on when we should consider exiting positions. Deciding when to exit a position, to a degree, may depend on your temperament. However, one goal of this book is to make sure you don't invest solely around your temperament and urges.

One thing about resistance is that it's often been tested previously as support (price bottom) in the stock's past, which points to emotions that may have previously swayed large swathes of investors and provided those large swings that turn losing stocks into winners and winning stocks into losers. Put another way, stock prices do seem to exhibit having a "memory" and stocks will often respect levels in the future that they've respected in the past. We'll discuss the impact of emotions on stock prices in the next chapter. For now, it's important that we recognize that emotions do have an impact.

Again, the fact of the matter is stocks usually trail where they should be changing hands. Yes, the stock market is not efficient. If it were, individual stocks and the overall market wouldn't experience such wild swings from time to time on news that's minor and not material in the grand scheme of things. Which means that stocks can be overvalued or undervalued at any given time.

Buying at current prices because we believe the stock is at a discount to likely future share prices is determined through **fundamental** research, but we want to be aware of these large swings that occur sometimes. We don't want to fight the crowd too long or risk facing short-term pressure that results in unnecessary losses. Having a basic understanding of charts is the first step in knowing when to act and when to show patience.

CHART FORMATIONS

Chart formations are wonderful snapshots of history and history in the making. It's like living in slow motion.

Everyone has thought, at one time or another, about the ability to go back in time. Using charts properly allows us the closest, realistic alternative. It allows you a chance to avoid stocks that are wrecks and gives you the opportunity to jump on board a huge move as it's lifting off.

As I mentioned before, there are many chart formations to go along with other signals and indicators. Most websites, even free sites, offer a large array of tools. Here are a few sites you can check out:

Trading Views - tradingview.com

Stock TA - stockta.com

Yahoo Finance - finance.yahoo.com

Google Finance - google.com/finance

My favorite chart formations are easy to identify, appear often and have been the most consistently reliable over all the years that I've been in the markets. It's really uncanny how predictive these formations are. They work over and over again.

I only want to cover three patterns in this chapter for your quick analysis but they each have a counterpart or a variation, so we'll actually look at each major pattern twice.

1. Double Top/Double Bottom

Double Top   Double Bottom

2. Head and Shoulders/Reverse Head and Shoulders

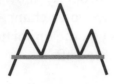
Head and Shoulders

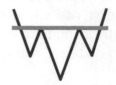
Reverse Head and Shoulders

3. Rectangles/Channels (the best to focus on for trading activity with short-term holding periods)

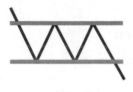
Rectangles

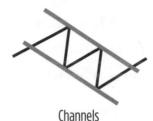
Channels

These are a few chart formations that I rely on to quickly and easily spot opportunities.

My goal is to keep the technical analysis quick and for it to maximize your fundamental work.

DOUBLE TOP/DOUBLE BOTTOM

Among my favorite formations are Double Tops and Double Bottoms because they're prevalent and have consistently delivered performance for me. Here's a quick view of what the formations generally look like:

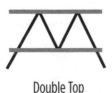
Double Top

Double Bottom

Quick note, I always begin my technical examination with a look at the past year, a 52-week chart, and then I adjust to a wider or more narrow view.

DOUBLE TOPS

I believe that Double Tops are absolutely the most important chart formation and one that must be recognized because it could save you money and preserve profits.

In CAT's chart above, the Double Top formation shows that after a rally, selling began to overwhelm buying and the stock pulled back. At this time, the stock had made a big move but possibly got ahead of itself. That established the first peak. The stock then pulled back (moved lower). It settled at a slightly lower level and then worked back higher towards the first peak. The stock again began to move up toward that previous peak. Investors in the stock, perhaps having missed the prior peak, began to close their positions. The result was that selling overwhelmed buyers once again. The formation is easy to see and is extraordinarily predictive.

Make a special note of just how dramatic the fall in CAT was after the Double Top formed. Failure to recognize this formation can be costly.

Fortunes have been made and saved by properly assessing and adjusting to Double Top formations.

Case Study

Micron Technology (MU) is a historically volatile stock known for amazing rallies and epic selloffs. This 2018 chart underscores a dramatic rally followed by a swift and short-lived pullback before the stock takes off again forming a Double Top.

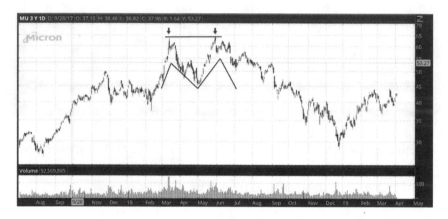

The failure to rally past the prior peak sent the message to those contemplating selling that the time was ripe. Shareholders that had enjoyed a very nice move up in MU from much lower levels, began to take profits. The result was a retreat in the share price that produced a near-perfect downtrending channel that didn't stop until after MU's share price was cut by more than half!

Some traders try to make money on each turn near each top and bottom of the trading channels but it's a difficult game and one best reserved for those folks with nothing else to do, like work or taking the children to soccer practice.

But these channels inform long-term investors and provide safeguards, especially when it comes to protecting profits and finding new entry points. Once a stock hits a resistance level and fails to take out a prior high point, the move lower can be swift and deep and, in the end, devastating for those that failed to observe the stock's changing price behavior.

Once the downside move occurs, it becomes difficult for investors to take the hit knowing the stock was just at a high point a short while earlier. So, mind games can often compound the mistake of not realizing the stakes that come when a Double Top is approached, established and leads to the price falling.

On the other side, breaking through a Double Top can send the underlying asset on a rocket ride higher. Still, be careful as I want you to make and bank money and not rely on hopes that make you undisciplined.

DOUBLE BOTTOMS

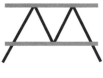

Double Top

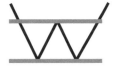

Double Bottom

The Double Bottom chart formation works just like the Double Top except in reverse. It's a great tool for predicting when to buy a financial instrument at a good price. Remember, the key to successful investing is buying low and selling high. The problem is that when stocks are getting cheap there are few mechanisms to know when it's cheap enough to buy.

The Double Bottom formation is a great tool to determine when selling is exhausted. It's an even greater tool when coupled with fundamentals that show a company shares aren't reflecting current or future value. As a reminder, we're watching to see if history repeats itself and the clues are already in place.

With a Double Bottom, the stock holds very close to where it held in the recent past and from where it rebounded previously. Because the potential rebound can have long-term implications, the ability to capitalize can be the difference between making some money in the stock market or making life-changing money in the stock market.

Case Study

Take a look at what happened after the S&P 500 formed an almost perfect Double Bottom in 2016. The S&P 500 is the main index used on Wall Street as a proxy for the stock market and, by extension, the economy (U.S. and outside the U.S.).

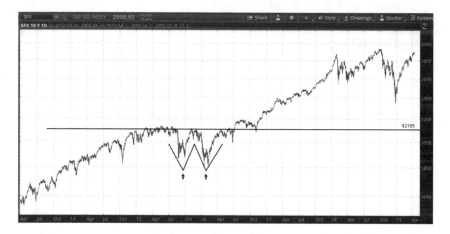

In early October 2014, the S&P 500 index stumbled to a just above 1800, which turned out to be a bottom. The S&P moved higher from there rallying to 2,126 in July 2015, just above the 2105 level, before stalling yet again.

The next major pullback took the index to a low near 1,810 on February 11, 2016, establishing a larger scale Double Bottom that held. The rebound eventually saw the index rally to 2,872 on January 23, 2018 for a gain of 54%.

By the way, I mentioned I like to begin with a one-year chart then expand and collapse the time horizon to gain greater nuance. A 10-year chart at the time of the Double Bottom formation would've given an investor greater confidence to buy the market and maybe additional names on their Watch List. It was clear that the rally that began from the March 2009 lows was still intact and very powerful.

HEAD AND SHOULDERS

Head and Shoulders

Reverse Head and Shoulders

Not only is this the name of a popular dandruff shampoo and a phrase for excellence that sets itself apart from the rest but it's also an important chart formation.

The standard Head and Shoulders is a bearish formation. This is something to consider when holding individual profitable positions in stocks. It can also help mitigate more losses in a stock that is a paper loss (unrealized loss, a stock you still have in your portfolio).

Head and Shoulders formations can pinpoint tops and Reverse Head and Shoulders are great at pinpointing bottoms.

Case Study – *JB Hunt Transport Services Inc. (JBHT)*

The example below is a Head and Shoulders formation for the chart of trucking giant JB Hunt Transport Services Inc. (JBHT):

On January 22, 2018 shares peaked at $125.00 a share and then promptly turned lower. The share price turned up again with the stock peaking at $130.00 on June 11, 2018 before pulling back again. The next push higher was a big test for the stock.

If the stock could climb above that June high point, it would be a major breakout. That didn't happen. Instead, the stock stalled at the same level as the January high point. These actions created a perfect Head and Shoulders formation, which is a great "sell signal."

January 22, 2018 Left Shoulder

June 11, 2018 Head

September 10, 2018 Right Shoulder

After hitting that right shoulder with a sharp move higher but immediately turning lower, the sell signal was established and fifteen weeks later the stock was down 28%.

Case Study – *Apple (AAPL)*

What we see above is a very good example of a Head and Shoulders pattern that appeared in Apple (AAPL) towards the latter stages of 2018. Apple rallied for most of the year and peaked initially near $230. It then backed off for about a month before finding support from which to launch another run towards the $230 high. It barely exceeded $230 and then retreated to a similar support level that it had after the first peak.

Peak 1 we'd identify as the left shoulder. Peak 2 then could become the head but we couldn't be entirely sure at that point. After dawdling around for another month, it tried another rally attempt but this one fizzled out well shy of Peak 2's high point and even lower than Peak 1's high. We had reason to become concerned and began thinking that Peak 3 of that failed rally could become the right shoulder.

Once Apple fell below the "neckline" where Apple's stock had found support over several months near $214, Apple's fate became technically sealed. Investors and traders realized that Apple's rally had lost steam after a "helluva" run higher for most of 2018. When combined with concerning news items, they began to shift aggressively into sell mode. The subsequent decline was breathtaking. The Head and Shoulders pattern that appeared was a harbinger of technical destruction.

Case Study – *Target (TGT)*

A very nice example of a Reverse Head and Shoulders can be seen in Target (TGT) below:

TGT began to trade in a range-bound manner in late 2015 and that persisted for nearly all of 2016. The lows in the mid to high $60's established in 2015 and 2016 gave out early in 2017 as support was breached. TGT tumbled below $50 in the summertime. These developments formed the left shoulder and head to that point. Late in the summer TGT began to rally from those lows and by late fall it had made it back towards the highs it established in 2016. It failed to push through and then spent months churning until reaching that high level again near $80 in the summer of 2018, all of which formed the right shoulder. It pushed above that resistance level, which again we'd call the neckline, and then tested it a few weeks later before finally rallying above $90.

RECTANGLES AND CHANNELS

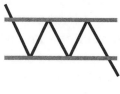

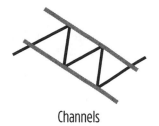

Rectangles   Channels

Rectangles and channels are visually very similar with the difference being that rectangles work in a horizontal fashion while channels are sloped. In both cases the price action unfolds and establishes lows and highs in a manner that's consistent with what the eye would expect.

Support and resistance levels persist and can be seen where they would be expected to appear. When stock prices move decisively above or below the established support and resistance lines, significant stock movement often develops.

Case Study – *Microsoft (MSFT)*

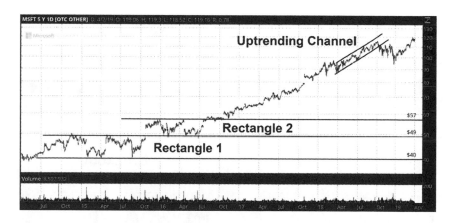

Notice how Microsoft (MSFT) leaves Rectangle 1 to the upside and then Rectangle 2 uses Rectangle 1's resistance level as its support level. MSFT eventually moved above

Rectangle 2's resistance level, began to treat it as support for over a month's time, and then was off to the races for nearly 2 years. Eventually, a very defined uptrending channel formed and MSFT's failure to hold support in that channel in late 2018 led to a selloff that clipped nearly $30.00 from MSFT's high point. Rectangles and channels indicate ranges of stock pricing. They identify trends in support and resistance. Channels indicate a direction other than horizontal in price action. These are important to recognize and pay attention to. As these two chart formations indicate, when a channel or rectangle are broken something significant is occurring and the smart investor starts investigating.

MULTIPLE CHART FORMATIONS

If you look at a long-term chart of any stock or ETF, you'll most likely see multiple formations that would've given you buy and sell signals over time. These technical formations reflect the natural flow of the market and individual stocks as investors respond to changing fundamental and behavioral factors.

The following charts of Lumentum and Verizon are good examples of this:

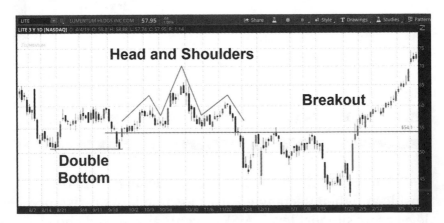

Looking at longer-term charts can help train your eye to spot these formations so you can take action when they give you the signal.

NOW YOU KNOW

I sincerely hope that these last 2 chapters have provided not only additional knowledge, but hope, clarity and excitement. I'm sure you've recognized how much you already know and how you're already "in the market." You should have already started or added to your Watch List.

You've gone through the quick fundamentals of the companies you're interested in, now it's time to conduct to a quick technical analysis to determine when to take action. Having all this knowledge won't create Unstoppable Prosperity - you must take action. You have to become observant, do research and learn to read charts. There are many ways to do these things and I've presented some of my favorites. Quick fundamental and technical analysis helps you build a solid Watch List. In order to more fully understand the risk and reward of every opportunity before you invest, I'll take you through a deep dive on fundamentals and technical in Chapters 8 and 9.

Below you'll find a list of actions to take that will help you implement what you've learned so far. I encourage you to take the time to go through them before you move on. You may even repeat them several times to make yourself more familiar with evaluating opportunities by doing effective research and looking at charts.

NOW EXECUTE

In this chapter, I've given you some key information on the initial technical factors you should consider and chart formations to watch for. Now it's time to apply that knowledge.

Start with your Watch List that you created after the previous chapter and take a look at the 52-week chart for each stock. Go through the following exercises:

- Identify and draw trendlines on the chart (support and resistance)
- Identify any specific chart formations that you've learned about in this chapter
- Identify what the historical formations signaled and when you should have gotten into or out of the stock
- Is there a formation building? Are there indications of what is likely to happen with the stock?

Remember, fundamental factors tell us what we want to buy. The technical indicators tell us when we should buy (or sell). Practicing this "quick look" technical analysis will help you know which stocks should move higher on your Watch List. The deep dive in Chapter 9 will help you know when to pull the trigger.

CHAPTER FOUR

BEHAVIORALS: MANAGING THE MOODS OF THE MARKET

In the last chapter, I provided you with tools to help you make *rational* decisions to reach your goal of Unstoppable Prosperity. These tools will allow you to manage and mitigate your own naturally occurring emotions, blunting their ability to influence your decision making as you encounter exogenous events with a knowledge of fundamentals and other factors.

It's one thing to be the master of your own emotions and avoid self-sabotage in your investing efforts, but it's something entirely different to weather the storm when everyone else seems to be losing their collective minds. In keeping with our goal, the next step is to learn how to make money from the mayhem of the *emotional* rollercoaster. To do that, it's helpful to understand why these emotional storms happen.

For a long time, there was a notion that the stock market was largely a rational exercise where buyers and sellers are matched daily. In an ideal world, some sessions would have a few more buyers than sellers or a few more sellers than buyers. There would rarely be an imbalance that derails the orderly reputation of the market.

This idea of markets being orderly is the basis of the Efficient Market Hypothesis. This theory states that asset prices are a full reflection of available information. Proponents of this investment hypothesis suggest that investors can't beat the market because so much information is available to the public and, therefore, built into current share prices. One would expect, with all of the technology and information now in the hands of any investor or trader who wants it, this would certainly be the case.

If this were true, would the stock market ever move more than 5% in a single session or 10% over a 48-hour period? If this were true, would an individual stock drop more than 10% in a session or 20% in a 48-hour period? We're talking about multi-billion-dollar reactions to "news" that often isn't new or, surprisingly, isn't based on changes to prior facts and trends.

The notion that markets are rational because people are rational falls short because people are irrational. In addition to that, the irrational behavior of a few can have a domino effect that triggers irrational actions in normally calm, rational people.

But when the waves of panic come... it's not about decisions, it's about reactions.

TOO MUCH INFORMATION?

Perhaps the greatest irony with respect to the notion of an efficient, rational market is the fact that there's never been more readily available information about individual companies and the market than is available right now. The availability and easy access to all this information provides the keys for individual, self-directed investors to level the knowledge playing field and realistically seek their own fortunes through investing.

However, just because this information is out there doesn't mean everyone has read it or that everyone understands what they've read. If the overall market is the sum of its components (investors), then it's safe to say 99% aren't clued in to the actual information and data and the meaning of that data.

In short, people don't read a lot of financial information and filings.

This might explain why the most manic periods of the market happened during the Great Depression or since 1987. All but one of the top 20 worst single day percentage losing sessions on the Dow Jones Industrial Average have occurred in just three periods.

In the entire history of the Stock Market, before the Great Depression, there had been 4 of those days. During the Great Depression there were 9 of the worst days, as you'd expect during the worst financial crisis in our history. But here's the interesting thing, 7 of those days have occurred during what we can call the "Information Era."

LARGEST DAILY PERCENTAGE LOSSES		
RANK	DATE	% CHANGE
1	10/19/1987	-22.61
2	10/28/1929	-12.82
3	10/29/1929	-11.73
4	11/06/1929	-9.92
5	12/18/1899	-8.72
6	08/12/1932	-8.40
7	03/14/1907	-8.29
8	10/26/1987	-8.04
9	10/15/2008	-7.87
10	07/21/1933	-7.84
11	10/18/1937	-7.75
12	12/01/2008	-7.70
13	10/09/2008	-7.33
14	02/01/1917	-7.24
15	10/27/1997	-7.18
16	10/05/1932	-7.15
17	09/17/2001	-7.13
18 (TIE)	09/24/1931	-7.07
18 (TIE)	07/20/1933	-7.07
20	07/30/1914	-6.91

Pre-Great Depression (before 1929)
Great Depression (1929 - 1939)
Information Era (since 1940)

Source: https://en.wikipedia.org/wiki/List_of_largest_daily_changes_in_the_Dow_Jones_Industrial_Average

That's right, since the buildout of the information superhighway providing a conduit to more information on publicly traded companies, there have been as many dramatic single day market swings as we saw during the turbulent times of the Great Depression. In fact, the biggest one-day swoon happened on October 19, 1987 almost 50 years after the Dow Jones Industrial Average crashed -10.57 points or 7.75% to close at 125.7 on October 18, 1937.

Based on what's currently happening in the market, some could argue there's too much information. I don't believe that to be the case. I've been in the market long enough to know its old reputation as being rational and efficient is wrong. It may have been at some point in the very beginning, and it may be again at some point in the future, but in the here and now it's not.

Investors must have a basic understanding of behavioral analysis because group reactions can run amok. You need to know what's driving these sharp spikes and swoons in order to determine, rationally, what you need to do to protect your growing wealth.

OH, BEHAVE!

In recent years the terms "Behavioral Economics" and "Behavioral Analysis" have become a prevalent part of market analysis conversations. But it's still largely a mystery, other than the fact that it exists and can have a lasting, long-term impact on investing efforts.

The main reason for the rising importance of behavioral analysis was the awarding of the Nobel Memorial Prize in Economic Sciences to Richard Thaler in 2017.

The Royal Swedish Academy of Sciences said Thaler's contributions "built a bridge between the economic and psychological analyses of individual decision making. By exploring the consequences of limited rationality, social preferences and lack of self-control, he has shown how these human traits systematically affect individual decisions as well as market outcomes."

I would add a note of caution here. Keep in mind that when we speak of "market outcomes" we're referring to short-lived events. They must not be allowed to have a detrimental, long-term impact on your portfolio. Later I'll show you how to manage your portfolio to negate "market outcomes" that might otherwise cause the less knowledgeable to take big losses.

But, back to the work of Richard Thaler. The world reacted to the news with open arms and with lots of questions, including many about the application of various theories behind his work.

Much of the foundation for Thaler's work began years earlier. Daniel Kahneman, an economist, and Amos Tversky, a psychologist, identified what they called the "Endowment Effect." This emotional reaction identified the emotions people attached to ownership. Their experiments included one in which recipients were given mugs and later asked to swap them for items of equal or even twice the value and, overwhelming, they held onto their mugs.

I've seen similar ownership issues with individual investors.

My epiphany on the power of emotions over logic and sound investment management came in the aftermath of the bursting of the tech/internet bubble. For several years after the bubble burst, I'd perform portfolio reviews that would be littered with names of stocks that were never coming back. Of course, emotions during the tech bubble were infinitely more intense than the ownership of a mug, but the principal was just the same. Investors placed an intrinsic value on some of their stocks that wasn't matched by the value of the company behind the stock. Their decision to hang on to these losing positions wasn't a rational but rather an emotional one.

Investors had been convinced they had the "next big thing" that was going to make them obscenely rich overnight. Everyone was going to retire in a few years and buy their own remote island somewhere.

That sense of *endowment* isn't the only emotion that can drive decisions. A large part of Thaler's work revolves around the concept of loss aversion. This concept dovetails nicely with the faulty notion that you never lose in the stock market until you sell. The fact of the matter is, the worst thing an investor can do is be victimized several times for a single mistake. Let me explain.

Let's say you made a bad investment and it crashes with no hope of rebounding. You can then compound that mistake by doing any one of the following:

- Refuse to sell
- Keep buying more at lower share prices
- Don't make any other new investments

This kind of behavior goes to the famous observation about "pride and ego" sinking investor efforts. Of course, psychologists say there are good forms of "pride" but when it blocks investors from acknowledging poor decisions and then compounding them with additional poor decisions, it becomes a dream killer.

But what happens when a lot of investors and would-be investors are all acting irrationally at the same time? The results are the wild swings we see in the market from time to time. Investors react, rather than act, often to the detriment of their portfolios. I never want you to be caught in this trap. There are times when a stock is worth an upswing or a downturn and you should be able to act in a timely manner. But when those swings are the result of "the herd" reacting without good information, you need to make smarter choices.

Upon winning the Nobel Prize, Thaler was quoted as saying, "economic agents are human, and that economic models have to incorporate that." Now, more and more professional investors are incorporating behavior into their models. But it's a lot easier said than done.

THIRD PILLAR

I recognize that the emotions of crowds and a series of mistakes can warp the stock market. This combination creates an almost irresistible trap for everyone to make the same mistake. Misery loves company and puts out one heck of a welcome mat. Let's avoid that invitation but stay aware of opportunities to be had when the masses are messing up.

Remember my Pillars to investing:

> **Fundamental:** tells us *what* to own and not own – allows us to find the best ideas based on factual trends and financial statistics.
>
> **Technical:** tells us *when* to own and not own a position – allows us to identify and incorporate historic moments of stress and opportunity.
>
> **Behavioral:** tells us when to hold a little longer for that extra "oomph" that adds up over the years or sell sooner than other signals might indicate to avoid being trampled by the herd.

Behavioral analysis attempts to measure the moment(s) when emotions have taken control of investor attitudes and actions, upsetting the typical balance of buyers and sellers. While the focus of behavioral analysis tends to be on the rapid decline of value in assets like stock prices, it can, and does, work both ways.

Stocks can move higher simply on the strength of the idea that they're going to move higher. This notion that "the sky's the limit" can spark demand. This increase in demand results in higher stock prices making that assumption come true. Sure, unless the underlying fundamentals are improving just as rapidly, the supply of buyers will eventually either dry up or there's news that casts doubt on the underlying value of the stock (the fundamentals). The result is often a sharp pullback.

This is another example of why understanding the fundamentals of any company whose stock you want to own is so important. If the fundamentals aren't changing, and there's no specific events that would cause the price of the stock to go up, there should be red flags waving all over.

The situation described above is the backdrop for behaviorists looking for stocks during excessive moves and overreactions in either direction. Let's take a look at emotionally driven moves with individual stocks beginning with parabolic moves to the upside.

For us that means that a stock that was moving on a chart in a nice, steady 45-degree angle upward suddenly takes off and goes up at a 60-degree or even a 90-degree angle. In other words, the stock goes from moving steadily higher to taking off like a rocket ship.

This chart of NVIDIA Corporation (NVDA) is a perfect example of what a parabolic move looks like. Pay particular attention to what happened after the parabolic upswing:

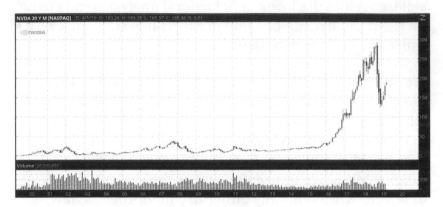

These parabolic moves demonstrate how behavioral, rather than fundamental or technical, factors impact an individual stock or industry. As you can see, these moves are not sustainable. They're exciting on the way up but devastating on the way down.

Sometimes stocks come to market with so much hype that the share price immediately becomes detached from fundamentals resulting in shares pricing at unrealistic valuations.

There are lots of ways to judge the value of the stock market and individual stocks. While I'm not a big fan of using Price to Earnings (PE) ratio in determining buy and sell decisions for individual stocks, there's no doubt Wall Street is obsessed with this valuation metric.

Historically, the average stock changes hands at a Price to Earnings ratio of 16 but it's hardly ever at that exact number. It's normally moving in a range that goes from 14 to 18 PE ratios. Stocks in fast growing sectors command higher PE ratios because they're normally growing revenue so fast and many times plowing it back into the business. In those cases, earnings aren't the top priority for the company.

Be that as it may, you should know where the PE is for stocks you own and have an idea of their own historic range to use as a benchmark in determining if they're too expensive or maybe inexpensive and a really good value.

For the broad market, it's good to understand that Wall Street gets antsy when PE ratios are above 18. However, once PE ratios move beyond 20 there's a sense that, while the stock seems "expensive," there could be more short-term movement to the upside.

These instant bubbles aren't just a lot of unsuspecting individual investors throwing caution to the wind. These buyers and traders include some of the most sophisticated players on Wall Street.

Considering there are more than 300 global unicorns (newly formed companies that are already privately valued at $1.0 billion or more) that will come to public markets soon, we're bound to see dozens of stocks go parabolic and then pullback. Some of these may eventually settle down and trade higher after fundamentals live up to the hype and generate renewed optimism.

We're also going to see lots of stocks make spectacular upswings, like Roman candles soaring through the air. These stocks may look like they have a date with the stars. Then, just as quickly, they'll fizzle, burn out and fall back to earth. All the hype, hope and excitement that was the hallmark just days and weeks earlier is gone.

But the ride, even if short, is so amazing it becomes a beacon. We all want to be a part of the winners and all want to make quick, easy money. Let's look at an example.

Case Study

The GoPro initial public offering was even more of a hot new offering than normal. The company was started by an adventurer who needed a way to film his underwater vacation. It became wildly popular in the world of action and adventure junkies.

Cameras mounted on helmets allowed everyone to skydive off cliffs, swim with the sharks and capture their own adventures on the local bike trail.

GoPro (GPRO) went public in June 2014 at $24 a share. It closed at $31 on the first day of trading and $38 the next day. The stock was hot! In July, management announced a new $399.99 camera resulting in a whole new round of hot buzz. On top of that, fundamentalists were justifying higher valuations based on the massive number of eyeballs on the company's website as well as the new content posted there.

All the pieces were in place for a parabolic move.

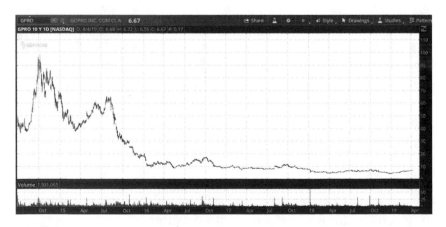

Volume is the most important tool for observing and trading parabolic moves.

Take note that I said *trading* since these moves are simply too volatile and violent for long-term investing, and better suited for that portion of your portfolio set aside for short-term trading.

Share price movement becomes a beacon that attracts more and more buyers. Soon, nobody is looking at technical or fundamental metrics anymore. It's pure excitement.

Some call this excited buying the "Greater Fool Theory." The belief is that an obviously overbought stock can be purchased because there will be greater fools following behind to pay an even higher price for the same stock.

I don't agree that individual investors buy into parabolic moves assuming there's a greater "fool." I think most are excited about a product or service and want to be part of the action. Once they buy that stock, it's like the coffee mug I mentioned earlier. They value it a lot more than anyone else and demand a much higher price to part with it.

Some investors, especially professionals, try to gauge parabolic moves using the Keynesian "beauty contest" theory. The thinking goes like this: if folks are asked to choose the six most attractive faces from hundreds of photographs, and they're told that those who picked the most popular faces would be eligible for a prize, the entrants would tend to ignore their own opinion of beauty and try to guess what the masses might find attractive.

The same can be applied to the market. Buyers ignore fundamentals and attempt to guess what the masses are willing to pay for a stock. This approach is too much guesswork for me, especially when I see former highs taken out on ever-increasing volume.

Take a look at the GoPro chart and description below:

At the start of August, shares of GPRO were moving sideways on light volume but toward the end of the month the shares began to pop, and volume began to surge. From August 11th to 27th the average daily volume was 2.6 million shares. The share price rallied from $38.00 to $45.29 during that period, creating strong momentum.

DATE	SHARE PRICE	VOLUME
08/28/2014	$48.90	10,600,000
08/29/2014	$51.80	10,250,000
09/02/2014	$53.94	9,100,000
09/03/2014	$56.86	9,200,000
09/04/2014	$53.08	8,200,000
09/05/2014	$58.75	7,600,000
09/08/2014	$63.52	12,000,000
09/09/2014	$64.19	13,400,000
09/10/2014	$68.47	12,400,000

On August 28th the stock traded 10.6 million shares and the price spiked to $48.90. The share price continued to rally higher. This is the buy signal for technicians (see first arrow).

The next big move came on September 5th when the stock rallied almost $6.00 on 7.6 million shares (still well above the 2.6 million average from the prior month).

On Sept 5th the stock took out the Sept 3rd high (see second arrow) which was a clear buy signal and the "momentum crowd" showed up. A behaviorist would tell you that success begets success, turning the stock parabolic.

TRADING PARABOLIC MOVES

The leg of the rally that saw shares of GPRO go from $37.65 on August 4th to $68.47 on September 10th was a classic example of a rally going from fundamental possibilities to technical buy signals to emotional buying. Throughout this process the question was when to ring the cash register. For me, the answer came on September 11th when 15,000,000 shares changed hands and the stock closed lower.

Admittedly, you could look at a stock having made such a huge percentage move in such a short period of time and think that a drop of less than a dollar wasn't a big deal. Indeed, the stock did move slightly higher after the drop. But when protecting individual positions, or your entire portfolio, during emotionally charged periods we need to match some art to our science. It's fine to exit early if you're making a lot of money or protecting gains and principle. The volume of shares traded, and the drop-in price was an indication to me that the emotions that had been driving the price upward were beginning to wane. It was time to take my gains. But let's follow the story of this stock just a bit longer.

THE NEXT LEG HIGHER

By now GPRO was a superstar stock and had captured attention from even casual market watchers but the volume settled after that 15 million share session. Remember, at this point my only guide was a surge in volume that took the shares to new highs.

DATE	SHARE PRICE	VOLUME
09/22/2014	$68.27	4,200,000
09/23/2014	$72.88	8,100,000
09/24/2014	$78.46	12,100,000
09/25/2014	$81.31	14,400,000
09/26/2014	$82.10	13,000,000
09/29/2014	$90.94	26,700,000
09/30/2014	$93.10	31,800,000
10/01/2014	$91.80	12,900,000

Shares of GPRO were drifting higher but the next **behavioral buy signal** occurred on September 23rd when shares surged more than four dollars on nearly double the volume of the previous session and took out the prior high point.

The next three sessions saw volume ratchet up to an average of thirteen million shares and the stock continued to move higher.

The parabolic move continued as momentum carried through the weekend. Monday, September 29th saw close to 27 million shares change hands as the stock rocketed more than eight dollars to $90.94 (see first arrow).

The next session saw a volume of 31,800,000 shares and the stock climb to $93.10 (see second arrow). If you were riding this wave you should've been looking for an exit ramp as excitement seduced previously reluctant investors into the stock.

On October 1st, close to 13 million shares traded but the stock slipped. That was the exit sign. GoPro's fortunes have only deteriorated ever since.

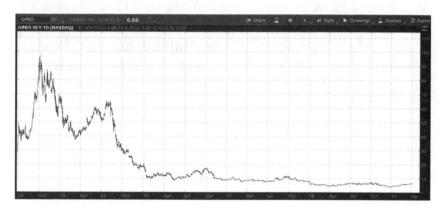

Remember when we used the volume signal to take profits on the prior high leg, even though the stock continued to move up? My decision was an example of taking profits and protecting my gains. Staying with the stock beyond that point involved increased risk. However, if you chose to do that, you should've used that same discipline on October 1st. Closing then would've allowed you to exit the position near the all-time high point. You would've made a profit and not risked taking a big loss.

I did recommend the stock as a **trading** idea after shares peaked. These parabolic moves continue even as the shares are losing altitude. However, the swings are large enough to make money as a trader.

GoPro is an example of a parabolic move upward. Let's look at the downside as well.

MARKET CRASHES

As we've seen with GoPro, upside behavioral moves happen when emotions (excitement and greed) lure additional money from the sidelines. When markets, or individual stocks, slip into freefall mode it's just a matter of shaking out current shareholders.

Moreover, downside moves are precipitated these days with machines and programs designed to panic rather than act as rational sentries against the emotions of humans. When freefalls happen, it's far too difficult to try to pinpoint what the actual bottoms might be and guessing like that is a dangerous waste of time. Here's a dramatic example of what I mean.

The market crash that began in 2007 and ran to 2009 stalled from time to time but never hinted at a buy signal until midway through 2009. Ideally, if you owned stock during that time, you'd have closed losers based on deteriorating fundamentals but held great stocks that were down because the market was down generally.

Exiting the market generally, or selling stocks with strong fundamentals, would've meant that you missed the rebound in 2009. You might've been willing to come back in later that year or early in 2010 but you would've left money on the table! By using my Pillars and sticking with your plan, you can maximize your profits even in turbulent times like we saw in 2008 and 2009.

NOW YOU KNOW

There are very few people that can contain their emotions when money is involved. This is why the same people win the World Series of Poker tournaments all the time. It's not that they get better cards, they just practice better self-discipline.

The great part of investing is that it doesn't have to be a game of chance. But from time to time, you need to recognize that you'll face emotional challenges outside your control.

Understanding what drives these behavioral events, and your options to mitigate your own personal losses and take advantage and make money from them, will be key components of taking you to your goal of Unstoppable Prosperity.

Let other people invest on their emotions. You can take advantage of their excitement and greed or their panic if you stick with your plan and apply my Pillars to your decisions.

One final note before taking action on this. You need to realize that there will be times when your own emotions will want to get into the act. It's only natural. Just be aware and force yourself to make decisions through knowledge and not emotions.

NOW EXECUTE

I want you to look at several stocks that either rose or fell very quickly in the last year. When you find them, do a quick internet search on each to determine if there was any fundamental reason for the change in stock value.

If there wasn't, look at the major news stories for the day the incline/decline started and determine if there was anything in the financial environment that might have triggered the change.

If nothing jumps out, you know you're looking at a purely behavioral reaction. Look at the length of the reaction and what the stock did when things settled down. It's a lesson to remember.

FIVE

CHAPTER

PORTFOLIO COMPOSITION AND MANAGEMENT

When you're a self-directed investor you're the Captain of your fate, the Master of your destiny, and with that comes big responsibilities. I still love that idea and challenge more than handing my money over to someone who over-promises and under-delivers.

Money managers and major Wall Street firms make billions of dollars annually ostensibly to navigate the ups and downs of the market, manage risk and achieve outsized returns.

These money managers have rarely beaten the market. This underperformance has led many to ask the same question, "Where are the customers' yachts?"

According to a 15-year study by Standard and Poor's ending in 2016, money managers struck out overwhelmingly when it came to outperforming the annual returns of the S&P 500.

MONEY MANAGER UNDERPERFORMANCE VERSUS S&P	1 YEAR	5 YEAR	15 YEAR
LARGE - CAP	66.0%	88.3%	92.2%
MID - CAP	89.4%	90.0%	95.4%
SMALL - CAP	85.5%	96.6%	93.2%

Source: https://us.spindices.com/documents/spiva/spiva-us-year-end-2016.pdf

I want you to manage your portfolio with two major objectives:

- Make money
- Manage risk

To do that effectively, you'll need to have a basic understanding of some concepts that might be new to you. Not to worry. I'll show you what you need to know. Let's look at the first concept.

ASSESS OPPORTUNITIES

If you do this wrong, or allow yourself to be overwhelmed, it could feel like a demolition derby. That frightens many people. They give up before they even start and just hand their investments to someone else. They pay the fees and accept the results. Then they wonder why they aren't reaching their goals.

When you do it properly, it puts you on the road to Unstoppable Prosperity. You're much more capable of handling your portfolio than you probably realize. By the end of this chapter, you'll have more confidence and knowledge to better handle your own portfolio and be on your way to reaching your goals.

For portfolios of $250,000 or less, I like the idea of dividing your funds in twenty different positions, all at the same dollar amount. So, for instance, if your account was funded with $100,000, you'd establish twenty different positions at $5,000 each.

If you average 10% annual returns over 25 years in this account, it would be worth $1,083,470 without counting dividend income. But our goal is to achieve larger gains. On that note, if you were to add $10,000 annually the 25-year total would be $2,165,288. Achieving that level of success is something you can do. If you've worked with a broker in the past, or if you've relied on mutual funds as your investment strategy, you need to see if they've performed that well for you. My guess is they haven't. It's time to take control and get what you deserve.

Standard & Poor's has divided the entire market into 11 sectors comprised of more specific individual industries:

1. Communication Services

2. Consumer Discretionary

3. Consumer Staples

4. Energy

5. Financials

6. Healthcare

7. Industrial

8. Materials

9. Real Estate

10. Technology

11. Utilities

I provide more detail later in the chapter about each of these sectors and the types of stocks that fit into each one.

Cash is the twelfth "sector" I use for my allocations. There are times to have exposure to each of these sectors and times to avoid them. There are also times you'll want to be very aggressive, which brings us to the weighting of your portfolio.

Below is one sample of a weighting allocation of 20 positions among the 12 different sectors:

Communication Services	Consumer Descretion	Consumer Staples
2	4	1
Energy	Financials	Healthcare
1	1	1
Industrial	Materials	Real Estate
3	4	0
Technology	Utilities	Cash
1	0	2

There are several macro factors that determine how much exposure you want, or need, to have in a specific sector. Let's take a look at those:

MACRO CONDITIONS

Things happen that are completely out of our control, but we must deal with them. When it rains, we reach for a raincoat and umbrella. Rain is just a short-term, typically uneventful, exogenous event that might make the day longer and slower but doesn't really interrupt our lives.

Of course, when I was growing up, we had umbrellas, raincoats and galoshes next to the door so we could adjust to the weather quickly. It gets a lot more complicated for businesses. They must envision, create and execute business plans over several continents, all with their own specific issues and macro conditions.

Rain may ruin a picnic but larger weather systems, from hurricanes to droughts, can drastically change things, often in the most profound ways. That's what businesses must deal with. And, because you'll be part owner of some of these businesses, the way management handles these conditions is of paramount concern.

The good news is we can sell our ownership stake if management isn't up to snuff. We need to be aware of these macro concerns because sometimes events are so enormous it goes beyond even management's abilities to maneuver.

These external macro events don't only come in the form of harsh weather. There are several external forces that may come at us slowly or seem to erupt from nowhere.

For businesses, the list of uncontrollable events and trends (macro conditions) is extensive:

- Societal (from what we eat to how we spend our time and money)
- Changes in laws (taxes and regulations)
- Demographic (populations age, shift and change over time)
- Political (in addition to legal changes there can be ideological changes)
- Technology (from moving mankind to allowing mankind to not move at all)
- Ecological (from cleaning the ocean to slowing the warming of the earth)
- Economic (GDP strength and weakness, employment trends, central bank policies)

All these macroeconomic conditions and inputs will influence the stock market and, as a result, your asset allocation.

The most prevalent macro condition to consider is the health of the economy. I'm sure it wouldn't surprise anyone to learn that the market comes down hard during recessions, which could mean lots of potential pain in your portfolio if you aren't paying attention. Let's look at a typical business cycle that contains both a recession and the stages of recovery. We'll begin by looking at recession.

RECESSION

Recessions are generally the result of the Federal Reserve action to deliberately slow the economy and tame inflation. Inflation is generally defined as being too much money chasing too few goods and services. It's an odd situation that the Fed must derail economic growth because people have too much money and are overpaying for things, but that's exactly what happens. Look at the chart below. Note that in each of the grey areas (recession periods) there's a drop in the market. I also want you to notice how short each of the recessions is, especially when compared to the upswings. Next time you hear someone talking about the risks of investing, remember this chart.

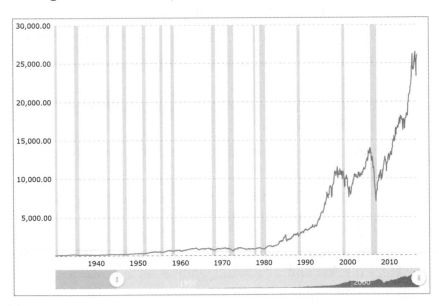

Recessions do mean a slower economy, slower profits and major changes in the dynamics of the stock market for a short period of time.

That also means you must make adjustments in your portfolio. But take care not to panic. Recessions are so short-lived (less than two years, often less than one year) and stocks tend to rebound sharply once the dust has settled.

There's no such thing as "recession proof" investing but there is "recession resistant" investing.

In order to have a recession resistant portfolio, you'll want to be "overweight" in certain sectors. When I use the term "overweight" I mean that you should have a larger portion of your portfolio in these sectors than you might for other conditions in the market.

Sectors to consider being overweight during recessions:

- *Consumer Staples* are a good choice because people don't stop drinking Coca Cola during a recession and more of them will shop at discount retailers and dollar stores.
- *Gold Stocks* should be considered. Some investors will make the move to gold, which is fine for a portion of your total investing dollars. But you need the liquidity of equities and dividend payments from owning stocks.
- *Utilities* represent a steady cash flow. We always pay our light bill even in the worst of times.

RECOVERY PERIOD

Following a recession, there's a recovery period. This consists of several stages.

The **Early Stage** comes immediately at the end of a recession. The economy starts to find its footing. People begin to buy stuff again and banking picks up as well.

Sectors to consider being overweight during this early stage:

- *Consumer Discretionary* (home improvement retailers)
- *Financials* (regional banks)
- *Health Care* (biotech has a solid track record of outperforming during the early recovery phase)

The **Mid Stage** is when the economy is hitting its stride and getting its groove back. This is generally the longest part of the recovery. It tends to see strong growth, which means stronger corporate profits.

Sectors to consider being overweight:

- *Technology*
- *Communication Services*

The **Late Stage** sees overall economic strength ebbing and greater signs of inflation.

Sectors to consider being overweight:

- *Energy*
- *Materials*
- *Utilities*

Note: Hiding out in cash is certainly an option during sharp recessionary periods. But it's essential that you take care and hold great stocks your research suggests will be higher in a year or so and into the future. The big goal is to not be victimized by gyrations in the stock market. But part of that goal must be to hang on to those future "Grand Slams" and not bail out of them because of a natural occurrence that only happens every 7 to 10 years. Careful research into the fundamentals will have given you good information upon which to base these decisions.

You may consider hedges like special ETFs (electronically traded funds) that move up in value as the market is moving lower. Here are two examples.

SH -Pro shares S&P 500 short

SDS -Pro Shares Ultra short S&P 500

You can certainly do additional research into these if you choose. The information you now have will allow you to make decisions to protect and grow your portfolio in any normal business cycle. But everyone wants to know about the "abnormal business cycle." Okay, let's take a minute and look at the extreme.

MARKET EXTREMES

It's difficult to know when the market has hit the exact tops or bottoms but it's not difficult to know when the market seems out of control in either direction. In **overbought** conditions, you need to acknowledge when your positions are changing hands at levels that seem too much too fast. When I'm in a winning position that starts to rocket up but earnings estimates stall for a couple of weeks, I become antsy.

When a stock or broad market is going into a parabolic phase, climbing straight up every single day without any news or any resistance, the chart shifts from a natural curve to a straight line higher. Selling during these periods means looking away for a period of time and resisting the urge to get back in because of the skyrocketing prices. This happened with marijuana stocks which rallied ahead of legalization in Canada.

Here's an example of what can happen with an overbought stock.

I interviewed the CEO of Tilray (TLRY), a Canadian medical marijuana maker, amid a parabolic rally. I eventually took to the air and social media to ask viewers to consider selling and taking their profits if they had already bought this stock. Some did but were upset as the stock continued to rocket higher. Of course, when the stock stopped rocketing higher it fell to earth like a meteor.

On July 30, 2018, the stock was trading around $24.00. In September, during this parabolic phase, it traded above $200. The stock rallied more than 500% in less than three months, but the sharp downturn caught some investors by surprise and they lost a lot of money. Folks holding for the top surely exited at lower prices than they would've gotten if they had been taking profits on the way up.

There are no hard and fast rules for scaling out of an investment that's gone parabolic. It's difficult to know the exact top and it's intoxicating to be in a stock that's making mind boggling gains every day.

While I hate using gambling references when talking about the stock market, there's a technique known as playing with the "house's money." This refers to taking all the money you began with and pocketing it with some gains. You then continue playing with the remaining profits (from the house).

This is what talk show queen Oprah Winfrey did with her investment in Weight Watchers.

When the deal was announced on October 19, 2015, shares of the stock were changing hands at less than $7.00. After an initial spurt it basically traded sideways. That is until June 2016 when earnings results began to live up to the hype. The stock began to trade higher and new highs beget new highs which attracted even more buyers. That, in turn, generated even greater excitement.

From June 2016 to June 2018 the stock took off from $27 to $108 for a 300% gain.

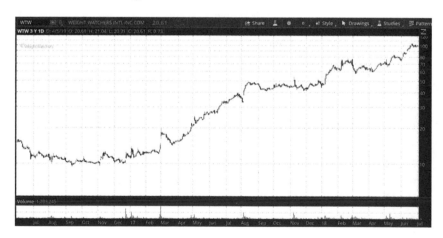

In 2018, it was reported that Oprah was doing less promotion with Weight Watchers and was focusing more on her own line of healthy foods through Kraft Heinz Co (KHC). Sales slumped with each new headline. On Feb 27, 2019, a disappointing earnings report sent the shares tumbling from $29 to $19 and headlines blared "Oprah Loses $50 Million Dollars". The news was dismal and unsurprisingly, it was received very poorly by investors. The stock's response was swift and devastating, which resulted in an overnight gap lower.

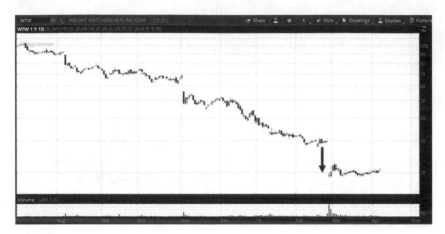

My reply was, "Don't cry for Oprah, she's made a mint on Weight Watchers $WTW."

She bought 6,362,000 shares at $6.79 and also exercised 3,513,000 options at $6.97 for a total cost of $69million.

Oprah sold $142 million worth of stock and donated 361,000 shares to charity as the stock was on the way up during its parabolic phase.

By the time this misleading headline and breathless commentary were made, there were clear facts. Oprah had already locked in 105% profit and was still sitting on a $62 million profit.

In other words, Oprah was playing with the house's money.

Obviously, this is an extreme example, but it does demonstrate the concept of "playing with house money."

The lesson to be learned is that it's critical to understand what is driving a stock's substantial growth and to make adjustments as there are any changes to those drivers. Oprah's involvement with WTW was a significant factor in their growth. When it appeared that she was becoming less and less involved, investors became increasingly sour in regard to WTW's prospects.

It's best to ease up on overbought situations like this and hold onto cash. Conversely, investors must make sure not to sell future grand slams when a market is in total freefall mode. Yes, during those periods, more than others, it's critical to close stocks where the value proposition has changed because those will be extra vulnerable holdings.

Again, do your homework and know the fundamentals of your positions. From time to time, you're going to have to decide on what to hold and what to sell. I don't want you doing that out of panic. Knowledge, not emotion, needs to be the tool you use.

HISTORIC VALUATION RANGES

Historic precedents play an important role in investing. Traditional valuation metrics, especially Price to Earnings ratio (PE), can be used as guides. The same is true with things like operating margins and growth rates. You need to be aware of these and use them to make decisions about the overall composition of your portfolio.

For the broad market, a degree of anxiety begins to creep in when the PE ratio gets above 20. This doesn't mean you should begin selling when the S&P 500 PE ratio is moving higher and cracks above 20. On the contrary, I think you should be fully invested and overweight in momentum stocks or High-Beta stocks (those trading at a higher volatility than the market in general) that will garner the most buying.

But this is the time to be prepared to close positions too.

During these periods, there'll be a parade of opinions complaining about the high PE ratio. This means the turn lower will be amplified by a chorus of voices predicting doom and the end of civilization as we know it. As we saw in the previous chapter, emotions can come into play and have a serious effect on the market.

So, be careful once the PE ratio peaks and begins to move back under 20. Take care to preserve profits and reassess ideas that were not rallying with the broad market because, more than likely, they'll be the biggest losers when the broad market tumbles.

On the flip side, the stakes are a lot higher when PE ratios are in freefall with the broad market. Generally, I like to see stability of the S&P 500 PE around 15 – that's when we start zeroing in on stocks that are seriously oversold.

S&P 500 Historical PE Ratio

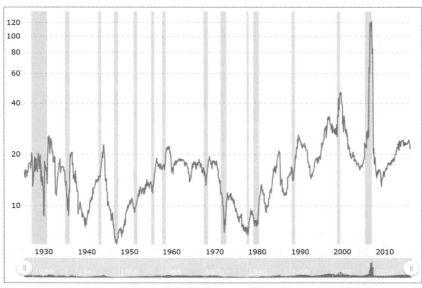

Source: https://www.macrotrends.net/2577/sp-500-pe-ratio-price-to-earnings-chart

There are numerous websites to see the historic PE ratios of individual stocks including Bespoke and Macro Trends. Use them as guides, especially when it comes to preserving profits. PE ratios are trends within the market, but there are other influences that we need to watch.

FEDERAL RESERVE

Over the years, the influence of the Federal Reserve over the economy and stock market has become extreme. It was great when Alan Greenspan, on the job as Chair of the Federal Reserve for only a month, stepped in to help the market recover from its Black Monday crash on October 19, 1987. Since then, the relationship has been contentious.

Part of the problem is the Fed talking too much. Expressing its intentions might be an effective tool and certainly has worked to jawbone the stock market lower. But it puts stocks in an unnaturally precarious position when it expresses a desire to lower equity prices.

When the Fed begins to hit the stock market or burst other financial bubbles (which they seem to miss during the inflating period), you should check your portfolio and be sure to own stocks in defensive sectors and increase your cash position. Defensive sectors are those that are thought to be *safer harbors* to be in when storms hit the markets. Sectors such as consumer staples and healthcare are considered to be defensive as they've historically held up better in major market selloffs. Think about it... corn flakes and antibiotics will still be consumed in nearly the same quantities even if the economy is slowing. Folks still need to eat breakfast and remain healthy!

Something else I need to mention has to do with the Fed. Investors must be careful to filter the noise around the Federal Reserve. It's only ratcheted up gyrations and volatility in recent times.

When the Fed is being "accommodative," cutting rates and implementing additional actions to spark the economy, it's a wonderful time to be long in stocks. Those sectors mentioned in the **early stage** and select momentum names are the areas in which to look for better than market performance.

"Weather forecast for tonight: dark."
~ George Carlin

I began this section talking about the rain and bad weather, but it's always been a convenient excuse for businesses that come up short, particularly those in the public eye. There's no doubt inclement weather changes consumer behavior, just as short summers or long winters can make supply and inventories an issue. These are mostly problems for the retail industry, particularly brick and mortar businesses.

Other businesses will hop on the weather excuse from time to time as well. I think of these explanations as the business version of "the dog ate my homework." Don't be fooled. If a stock you own is missing projections and management is talking about weather conditions, it's time to take another look at the fundamentals.

The most interesting part of measuring companies and their execution during adverse or rapidly changing macroeconomic conditions is that it provides the best backdrop to zero in on the best investments. The action of the underlying share price helps with this process. I'm always looking for the name in an industry that has the best performing stock - even when all of the stocks in that sector are lower. In other words, "Who is doing the best when everybody seems to be slipping?"

Great businesses take market share in bad times.

When investors are anticipating big macro changes, they have the ability to see how companies performed and how their underlying shares reacted. It's a wonderful time for taking positions and, in many ways, making money actually becomes easier.

MARKET SECTORS

In this section, I'm going to explain the 11 various market sectors and what types of stocks make up each. There are also unique Exchange Traded Funds (ETFs) that divide the S&P into eleven index funds that represent each sector. The symbol for each ETF is listed by the sector name below.

1. Communication Services
2. Consumer Discretionary
3. Consumer Staples
4. Energy
5. Financials
6. Healthcare
7. Industrial
8. Materials
9. Real Estate
10. Technology
11. Utilities

Remember, I consider *cash* as a twelfth "sector" for my personal portfolio allocations.

Communication Services (XLC)

- Diversified Telecommunication Services
- Entertainment
- Interactive Media and Services
- Media
- Wireless Telecommunication Services

This is a rebranded sector that includes a lot of high-flying names associated with technology like Netflix, Amazon and Facebook. This is a sector you want exposure to when the broad, global economy is growing and there's pricing power among American customers because they have more disposable income. The wild gyrations in the sector mean greater profit goals and larger potential losses. Because of the volatility of many of the stocks in this sector, it's easy to close these names too soon when we see a downturn only to see them quickly reverse.

The sector isn't known for dividend yield but has a lot of influence (10.2% of total S&P 500 weighting) because of all the famous high-flyers.

Consumer Discretionary (XLY)

- Auto Components
- Automobiles
- Distributors
- Diversified Consumer Services
- Household Durables
- Internet and Direct Marketing Retail
- Leisure Products
- Multiline Retail

- Specialty Retail
- Textiles, Apparel and Luxury Goods

Investors want exposure to this sector when consumer sentiment is good against the backdrop of a strong employment situation and wage gains. This sector is notorious for defined winners and losers. Pay close attention to market share gains and cost management.

Consumers often focus spending in different areas depending on the overall economy. For example, as new car prices go up, and the economy turns or flattens, looking into auto parts retailers is compelling. People will be holding on to their old cars a bit longer.

Something else to consider is that the big brick and mortar retailers have become very cyclical as they compete in an Amazon world.

Consumer Staples (XLP)

- Beverages
- Food and Staples Retailing
- Food Products
- Household Products
- Personal Products
- Tobacco

This is a defensive sector of companies that were household names in your great grandmother's home. They don't grow very fast so it's advisable not to pay too much for a dollar of earnings. By the same token, the sector is known for its solid cash flow and can be the perfect haven in concerning times while still earning money from solid and dependable dividend yields.

While many consider these products to be inflation-proof, intense competition keeps pricing power in check. From time to time, higher commodity inflation can be a drag on sales and margins, although those are often very cyclical events.

Energy (XLE)

- Energy Equipment and Services
- Oil, Gas and Consumable Fuels

Energy is self-explanatory and mostly moves up or down with the price of crude oil. But the price of oil has gotten more complicated over the years in part due to fracking technology. This technology has elevated the United States to the top producer spot. Beyond the excitement in U.S. investment options, the price of oil itself waxes and wanes in a very tight range based on the global economy and perceptions of where the global economy is heading.

I like the major oil companies that pay a steady dividend (the sector has the third highest dividend yield) and domestic companies in hot areas like the Permian Basin for trading ideas. For years, this sector had the most influence over the stock market and got a lot of attention from politicians looking for a piece of the action. Although that's quieted down, there's still periodic opposition and regulation risk.

Financials (XLF)

- Banks
- Capital Markets
- Consumer Finance
- Diversified Financial Services
- Insurance

This has become a very complicated sector to invest in since the onset of the Great Recession when it was the largest and most influential sector in the market. The index hadn't completely recovered even ten years after peaking (see the chart below). And some of the larger, so-called money center banks, like Citigroup and Bank of America, are significantly below their all-time high trading levels.

The big banks are supposed to mint money hand over fist in higher interest rate environments but that isn't automatic anymore.

Regional banks are compelling but need more regulatory relief after being made to pay for the sins of their larger brethren who created the Great Recession.

Insurance companies, brokerage firms and diversified financial services have been better investments, but the feeling is that big banks will rebound one day. One lingering problem for insurance companies and brokerage firms is the opaqueness around these companies and the complexity of understanding their risk.

Health Care (XLV)

- Biotechnology
- Healthcare Equipment and Supplies
- Healthcare Providers and Services
- Healthcare Technology
- Life Sciences Tools and Services
- Pharmaceuticals

This is a varied sector but there are several commonalities including strong balance sheets and steady pricing power. Health care, in general, is being driven by aging Baby Boomers, which should mean unique windfalls. However, there are some concerns. Politicians are looking to curb costs associated with health care from drug pricing to insurance coverage and reimbursements. Those are areas that will need to be watched.

This group tends to outperform in higher interest rate environments. In 2018, it became the most influential sector in the S&P.

Industrials (XLI)

- Aerospace and Defense
- Air Freight and Logistics
- Airlines
- Building Products
- Commercial Services and Supplies
- Construction and Engineering
- Electrical Equipment
- Industrial Conglomerates
- Machinery

- Marine
- Professional Services
- Road and Rail
- Trading Companies and Distributors

This is another very broad sector that's sensitive to the broader economy, business investment, lower interest rates and government spending and regulations. Aerospace and defense should hold up nicely as the next century sees the rise of Asia economically and militarily, bringing a new arms race.

The airlines and railroads are great proxies for the U.S. economy and, in fact, are better measured in the Dow Jones Transportation Index, which is useful in corroborating the health of the economy and veracity of stock market rallies. It provides another data point for the smart investor.

Information Technology (XLK)

- Communications Equipment
- Electronic Equipment, Instruments and Components
- IT Services
- Semiconductors and Semiconductor Equipment
- Software
- Technology Hardware, Storage and Peripherals

This is the most influential sector in the market. Technology has been a hot place for investors for several decades... sometimes too hot. Most investors are aware of the meltdown in technology stocks, which in many ways neither the stock market nor consumer sentiment has recovered from yet. But there are so many exciting things flying off the drawing boards and into our lives that everyone wants a piece of the action.

This sector is known for boom and bust cycles, especially computer chips, disk drives and other hardware offerings. With that boom and bust habit, this sector creates amazing buying opportunities from time to time and amazing challenges for investors on the wrong side of a trade.

Materials (XLB)

- Chemicals
- Construction Materials
- Containers and Packaging
- Metals and Mining
- Paper and Forest Products

Basic materials have become a small part of the S&P, only 2.7% total weighting. I wouldn't be surprised to see it altered or components shifted elsewhere. There was a time when containers and packaging were proxies for the entire economy. There's only a small amount of that today. The group does generally pay solid dividends.

Real Estate (XLRE)

- Equity Real Estate Investment Trusts
- Real Estate Management and Development

This is a great sector for investors seeking income through a real estate investment trust, or REIT. Most pay out 90% of gains in the form of dividends. Individual REITs can give investors specific exposure to industries such as retail, historical and industrial real estate.

Utilities (XLU)

- Electric Utilities
- Gas Utilities
- Independent Power and Renewable Electricity Producers
- Multi-Utilities
- Water Utilities

The ultimate safe haven, these stocks are steady dividend payers and occasionally there's outsized appreciation of capital as well. For the most part, however, I consider the sector to be defensive, a place to hang out in times of uncertainty – perhaps long enough to get a dividend payout.

Now that you understand the sectors of the market, let's examine the life cycle of an investment.

THE LIFE CYCLE OF AN INVESTMENT

Upon buying a stock, you begin a life cycle where each step comes with its own set of challenges. In that respect, buying is the easiest part of investing. I want to take this opportunity to reiterate that buying one stock and seeing how it goes before buying additional positions will defeat the purpose of investing in the first place.

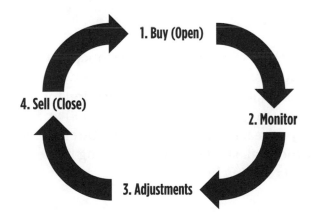

1. Buy (Open)

2. Monitor

3. Adjustments

4. Sell (Close)

1. BUY (OPEN)

This is where you buy the stock. The considerations include: how many shares to buy, how much to pay and exposure to a sector which comes with specific challenges.

Position Size

Buying approximately the same dollar amount of each stock you hold is your best hedge against the impulse of going for broke. In the example I gave previously, if you have a $100,000 portfolio, I suggest you have 20 positions of approximately $5,000 each. It's about position size and percentage of your portfolio, not the specific number of shares. One goal with your investing experience is to make it less like a casino and more a "thought-out game plan" with achievable long-term goals.

A basic mistake made by 99% of new investors and 98% of "seasoned" investors is going for that homerun. When it strikes out, it can wipe out a lot of good work and may even erase prior profits made in other positions.

Moreover, when investors take these kinds of big swings it consumes time. Time that would best be used to monitor other positions in the portfolio.

Buy in Tranches

In down markets I suggest buying in tranches, perhaps five entries at 20% of your normal allocation or two entries at 50%. For example, if your normal allocation for a position is $5,000, you may enter the position $1,000 or $2,500 at a time until you reach the full allocation. Often in major broad market swoons all stocks get hit, including those that are otherwise screaming buys.

Because bottoms are hard to pinpoint exactly (I've always said if you picked the bottom you're either lying or lucky, which is a little harsh but...) and because you know there's unrealized value in the stock tumbling with the rest, it's a lot less mental wear and tear to scale into the position.

I caution against buying during sessions when the major indices (Dow Jones, S&P 500 and NASDAQ Composite) are down one percent or more. Once you've decided to buy in tranches, how should you do it?

Purchase Method: *Buy Limit Order* (stock is bought at a specific price or better) since you're being selective, and time is on your side. The only drawback is that these orders are not guaranteed to be executed. But when the broad market is edging lower, take the time and get the price you want.

I know some are saying, "Why not wait until there's general stability in the stock and/or general market?" If you wait and "let the smoke clear," the stock will probably be at a price a lot higher than you could have achieved if you had used a Buy Limit Order and purchased on the way down.

Buy the Entire Position at the Same Time

I have no problem chasing fundamentals but in up markets, with a stock that has hit all facets of our buy signal, you shouldn't hesitate or get cute. These days, when there's a general sense that the train is leaving the station, the crowd rushes in quickly.

Your goal is to be there before the crowds. If you do this work correctly, you're going to be amazed how many times you take a position and, just days later, a major firm on Wall Street upgrades its ratings on the same stock.

Purchase Method: *Market Order* (stock is bought at current market price) means you'll more than likely get "filled" and own the stock. There can be an issue with the price you achieve when you lock in but we're trying to move before the crowds arrive. Make sure the firm you're using makes the effort to get you the best prices for Market Orders.

2. MONITOR

I want you to know how your portfolio is performing but I don't want you to be too myopic. It's easy to become so focused on your portfolio, especially during manias and panics, that you lose sight of your goals and overall plan.

The amount of time you spend looking at your portfolio depends a lot on your objective in the first place. If you're trading, you need to see those quick moves to capture them. If your goal is longer-term investment and appreciation, you might drive yourself crazy watching each tick.

By monitoring news you'll have some idea what's moving shares but often you'll have to connect several dots. Often what's moving your holdings around has nothing to do with fundamentals. For the most part, I think long-term investors need to use systems that alert them to daily moves in their own personal holdings of half of one percent or more.

Monitoring Tools

Most smart phones come with built in apps to monitor the stock market and for extra fees you can get all the bells and whistles you need. Your trading platform may also offer an app or you can find many helpful tools in your app store – regardless if you're an Android or Apple user.

With any of these tools there's one question that still remains.

What am I looking for?

Let's go about answering that now.

Intriguing Movement

When a stock is trading in a manner that's opposite its rivals, it's a sign something is going on. Obviously, when you're long a stock and it's down but its rivals are trading higher, it's time to leap into action and find out why.

1. Check volume (the number of shares that changes hands during a given day) – always check volume first and extrapolate to figure out what the total will be at the close of the session. When its clear volume is above the daily average, there has to be a greater sense of urgency.
2. Check market news sites
3. Check the company's website
4. Check Google News
5. Check brokerage rating changes
6. Check on peers (often bad news for one will influence the share price of the entire industry)

If there's no news, then you can be sure there will be in the next 24 hours and, more than likely, extend the directional move. I don't want you to panic but be prepared to update the fundamental value proposition and understand what the cause might be.

Next, look at technical implications. What have the trends been? What is the broader market doing?

While the goal is long-term wealth accumulation, one of the most devastating emotional hits you can take is a winner of 5%

or more turning to a loser. If that happens overnight and a stock gaps down, there's nothing you can do. But if you watch a stock slowly lose steam as earnings estimates begin to drift and key technical points are violated, you need to close the position.

If the move is from a brokerage downgrade, check out the rationale. I've found most downgrades based on a stock having made a big move are poorly timed. I don't let that influence my thinking, especially if the target remains the same. After all, this is how analysts get to have their cake and eat it too. If the stock resumes its upward move, the analyst can always say, "I had a buy rating" and if the stock pulls back, they can say, "We got out at the top."

Conversely, beware of analysts that got it wrong and continue to ignore a stock moving higher.

This is where behavioral analysis comes into play. Nobody is as emotional as analysts on the wrong side of a stock, especially if their rating isn't a "buy" and the stock is soaring. What normally happens is they might move from a "sell" to a "hold." But even in the face of a soaring stock they won't say the stock is a "buy."

If the reason the stock moved lower is news that reflects a material change in fundamentals, then you must make a quick reassessment.

If pressure on your position is from bad news with one of the company's rivals, it gets a lot trickier. One reason it's tricky is because companies with bad news tend to do three things:

- Make excuses (weather, currency, government turmoil)
- Don't come completely clean about issues and problems
- Throw the entire industry under the bus

Therein lies the problem. The stock you own might be the real reason their rival's shares are getting hit so hard. Companies all do the same thing when they post or report disappointing news. The report begins with a superlative headline then an admission of missteps and shortfalls that are normally blamed on exogenous events suggesting the issues were out of the control of management.

That explanation always suggests the problem is an industry issue. That's not always true but I don't expect a company to admit its losing market share to a rival.

This requires a review of historic execution and to return to your peer review (which I explain in more detail in Chapter 8). This isn't an automatic reason to sell, but the position must be watched closer.

You want to see if the stock you own is growing faster than its rivals on the top line and with margins. If you know this to be true, then you'll be cautious and avoid knee jerk selling when the entire industry or sector is lower on the bad news of one individual company that has thrown everyone under the bus.

3. ADJUSTMENTS

Share prices are going to fluctuate and you're going to have to deal with that movement keeping one thing in mind: the dollar value of a share does not determine whether a stock is expensive or not. Let me give you an example.

XYZ stock at $55 a share is potentially a different company than XYZ at $56 and certainly a different company at $66 a share. But this doesn't mean it's more expensive in either case per se. In fact, it could be less expensive. I'm not big on traditional valuations but I pay closer attention when I'm long on a stock that's become a sizable winner.

As Price to Earnings ratios rise, there will be greater temptation for Wall Street to downgrade the stock. I don't want you to close a position based on when the Street will downgrade the stock but be aware.

If a stock is in major rally mode, AND the fundamentals continue to improve, you might consider buying even more.

Yes, this goes against my rule about loading up, but there are times a grand slam becomes even more attractive at higher prices and there's a way to take advantage. What I'm doing in this situation is *chasing fundamentals*.

The trick here is to treat this as a completely new idea. Even imagine it has a different stock symbol. Later in this chapter, I'll show you how to manage your portfolio on the rare occasions you buy more of a stock that's higher. It will count as a separate position.

4. SELL (CLOSE)

There are two main drivers that cause you to close a position - taking losses or taking profits.

Taking Losses

There's no hard percentage I automatically use to close long-term buy and hold ideas so it's critical to be honest about what the data is telling you. You can be down a lot in a stock and you'll regret it if you take that loss and see it going across a ticker later at a much higher price, even if it's years later.

Never make promises to yourself to stay in a stock that's gotten hammered until it recovers. Most times it won't recover, and if it does, it won't be enough to make up for the losses. If it starts to come back, you'll replace your old promise of getting out with a new one that has an exit at a higher point. This isn't unlike promising to start a new diet on Monday after blowing it every Tuesday.

Never give up on my strategy. Trust it. It's not foolproof but it's proven, and it works.

Knowing when to exit a position is the hardest part of the investment cycle. It's so fraught with second guessing it can kill your long-term investing goals. Selling isn't universal but I have certain rules:

- *Never look back in regret after selling a position.* Use every move as a learning experience.

- *Never swear off the stock market because you lost money.*

- *Never take shortcuts after taking a large loss.* There's an undeniable urge for us to correct mistakes as soon as possible. For many investors, this means finding the next hot trade or investment. After the 2001 crash, many investors began loading up on stock options in desperate attempts to get it all back quickly. Some got into flipping real estate and some even rolled the dice with things like the Iraqi Dinars, thinking it would pop after the war.

- *Never average down more than once on a position in any 52-week period.* Averaging down occurs when we've already purchased some stock, the price drops and we decide to purchase additional shares of stock. If the price continues to decline from there, you need to reevaluate your outlook on the stock and if you should stay in the position.

- *Never stop following a company and its stock after selling it unless it became an unmitigated disaster and maybe not even then.* I've seen companies live up to their potential years later. With my approach, you're encouraged to really get to know the business from its very beginnings through the historic ups and downs.

A huge mistake seasoned investors make all the time is buying a stock that has stopped moving, is moving in the wrong direction or where the underlying fundamentals of the company never improved. They rationalize this as "being too early."

I've been early many times in my career. Those times I either make less money than intended or waited and took bigger losses than I should have. It's easy to look back years later and think, "I should have held that stock." It's much harder in real time and real life.

My favorite personal story of being early to discover a grand slam is Nvidia, which pioneered video game chips but was a cult stock before it became a household name.

I wanted my subscribers to own the stock long term when I initially identified its potential. It turns out the journey was much longer and, for the most part, we made incremental profits in a stock that mostly traded in a tight trading range until it crashed. Here are the times I featured it as a new, long idea:

- May 14, 2002 - We made money
- July 29,2004 - We lost money
- Mar 21, 2007 - We made money
- June 25, 2007 - We made money
- Feb 2, 2010 - We lost money

We made money most of the time we featured the stock, but it was never the rocket ship I anticipated it would be. The company had buzz in all the right places but might have had chip technology that was too early for applications beyond the niche area of high-speed gaming.

I've told this story many times but it's a perfect lesson in investing and how long it can take for hype to morph into reality.

My personal discovery, which never could breakout, finally got the attention of the smartest investment magazine in the business. On January 7, 2008, Forbes featured NVIDIA on the cover proclaiming it "Company of the Year."

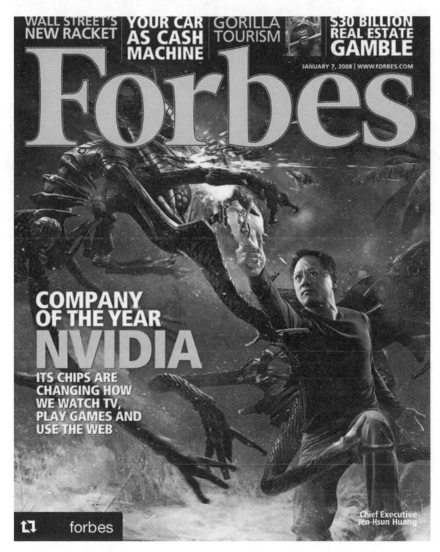

The shares were changing hands at $26.90 when the magazine hit newsstands but by the end of the year was changing hands at $8.62. Then came the spikes in the stock that took the stock to $18.68 in the winter of 2009 only to plunge again to $9.39 by August 2010.

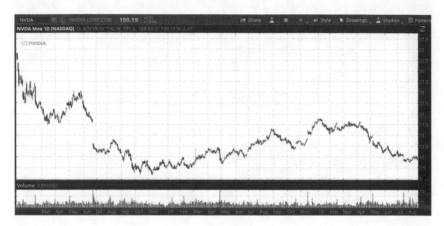

The stock finally broke out and truly began living up to the hype. On April 25, 2016 the stock broke out through $35 and made a moon shot to $280 by August 27, 2018 for a rally of 700%.

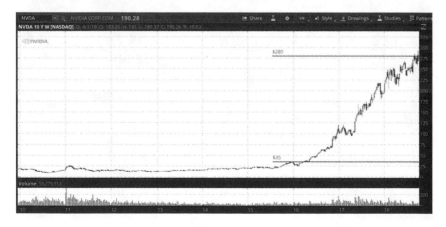

If I would've held onto the stock from the Feb. 2, 2010 entry and sold at the top in 2018, it would've been a 16,500% gain. Because of gyrations I stopped buying the stock with the intent to hold but instead with the notion of taking advantage of wild swings. I deliberately traded the stock 19 times from Feb. 2010 through 2018.

Special note here on High-Beta stocks. Earlier I used the term "High-Beta stock" and provided a brief explanation. Here's a more complete one.

A Beta of 1.0 means a stock trades with the same volatility as the broad market. In other words, the stock typically moves in similar percentages compared to the general market. It isn't doing anything way outside what we would expect from the market.

A Beta above 1.0 underscores the fact that the stock is trading in wilder gyrations than the broad market. Its volatility is more than we should expect to see in either direction. Simply put, it's more volatile than the broad market.

The implication is that when the broad market is doing well, these stocks could be doing great. Conversely when the stock market is edging lower these stocks could be in freefall. Moreover, these days stocks that move higher quickly attract more money from funds and investment approaches designed to be long stocks with lots of buyers.

Sounds like easy money and it can be but when selling occurs these same funds and programs are designed to reduce their positions as well. This exacerbates the volatility and extends big moves in either direction.

It's important to remember that owning High-Beta stocks like NVIDIA, or any of the other high-flyers, presents an awfully tough dilemma when they're moving against us and we're rapidly losing money. Hold them and you may risk even bigger paper losses (unrealized losses) or sell them too soon, and in a short period of time, we could be filled with regret after they've rebounded.

You must be prepared to take larger-than-generally-acceptable losses on High-Beta names. You must truly be prepared to trade them for short-term gains or endure paper losses waiting for them to rebound. These are super exciting names, but the hype usually comes long before the reality.

Taking Profits

Our goal is long-term wealth accumulation and there are going to be times you own certain stocks for many years but there will also be times when you take profits much sooner.

A general rule of thumb is to use a mental stop loss when a position is up more than 10%. This doesn't mean automatically closing the stock, but the value proposition has to be reevaluated.

There will be "tells" on when to close positions including:

- Earnings beating the Street by smaller margins
- Earnings misses
- Management warnings
- Profit margin expansion slowing or reversing
- Stock acts toppy (review charts and look for abnormal volume)
- Stock begins to give up gains during positive sessions to its peers and broad market
- Industry slowing and more rivals missing Wall Street consensus and lowering guidance
- Board market slowing and reversing

EMBRACING THE LIFE CYCLE

Being a successful investor is not just about buying the right stocks. Your financial future is much too important to "set it and forget it." Once you buy a good stock, it's imperative that you monitor your position and make necessary adjustments in order to manage your profits and losses effectively. The life cycle of an investment may seem daunting but the more you go through it, the more comfortable you'll become with the process. It's not nearly as time consuming as most people imagine. The small investment of your time now will have a significant impact on building Unstoppable Prosperity.

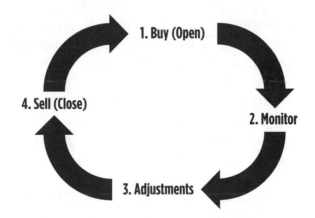

NOW YOU KNOW

Managing your portfolio effectively is essential in achieving your goal of Unstoppable Prosperity. I believe that to do so you should apply all three of my Pillars when making any decision to add stocks or close out a position.

There's an old saying, "Nobody ever went broke taking a profit." It's really a cop-out for closing a position in a moment of confusion and anxiety. Keep in mind, stocks go down faster than they go up so limiting your gains with guess work means the losers will have an even larger negative impact.

You won't go broke, but you could limit wealth creation and that's the exact opposite of the goal you've established.

Knowledge, patience and doing the work are all vital elements in successfully building and maintaining your portfolio. You may find it helpful to come back to this chapter from time to time as you see the market changing. Use the information about how the market acts to position yourself to your greatest advantage. After all, it's why you're in the market in the first place.

NOW EXECUTE

Effectively managing your portfolio must be an intellectual, not emotional, activity. Review your current positions to see if any of them have had a recent move. If so, dig in to see what may have caused it. You may find that there's no reason to do anything at this time, which is a good thing. That means your positions are working for you. If none of your holdings have had a recent move, research other popular stocks that have so you can still go through this exercise.

Look at what might have caused the move. Review fundamentals, check macro conditions, look at other stocks in the sector. Try to pinpoint the reason(s) for the move.

Determine what you need to do with these stocks, if anything, and when. Do you see the move as a buy or sell signal? Should you continue to hold your position? Write out your reasoning for that decision. Writing it down will help you be sure that you aren't acting on emotions but rather on hard facts. Rely on your head, not your gut.

SIX

OPTIMISM IN A WORLD OF INEVITABLE CORRECTIONS AND MARKET CRASHES

Markets and individual stocks have a history of correcting, which is a technical term for pulling back more than 10% from a recent peak. It's a naturally recurring part of investing and happens for a number of reasons, including reasons that often have nothing to do with the individual stock or even the stock market itself.

Stock market crashes, where there's more than a 20% pullback, are much less frequent. But the fear of losing everything in a stock market crash is the number one stated reason why millions of people resist becoming owners of companies that they personally support with their hard-earned money.

For investors, the psychological pressures of knowing corrections and crashes are inevitable lead to a ton of mistakes that can be avoided or mitigated.

WINNING ATTITUDE

Our approach to life, in many ways, will influence how we handle stock market adversity. You have to have a great attitude and retain a certain amount of optimism or you'll sell low and buy high more than you buy low and sell high.

I write about the stock market every day pointing out observations that go beyond the headlines that pop up on smartphones. So, when there's some event like more new 52-week lows than 52-week highs or stocks reacting to news or developments that seems to be the antithesis of conventional wisdom, my pessimistic friends and acquaintances give me a hard time.

I'll get an email saying something like, "Hey are you finally getting bearish? You're too optimistic." Questions and statements from friends or colleagues who always seem to be negative or bearish I find unfortunate. These professionals are supposed to be making people money. They also make me sad because of the impact they have on the wider audience who take them to heart.

It's great to be skeptical and to ask questions. It's what I do with every tick of every session whether up or down. But following perennial pessimists that make money anyway from newsletters, or analysis in ivory towers will leave you broke. Many people are waiting for the good old days that probably never existed or never will again. Dynamics of the market have changed, although in the end great stocks eventually outperform because they represent great companies.

It's important that you understand the underlying feelings driving the pessimists.

These kinds of comments are especially common from my buddies in Europe or other parts of the world. It's fine to listen to other voices, but I resent the notion of being too optimistic and will never allow anyone to curb my enthusiasm. I'm a realist and I've lived through market crashes and corrections, so I know they happen.

My pessimistic friends are realists too in their own way. Just not in a way that I think will help them reach Unstoppable Prosperity.

I like watching foreign movies as a counterbalance to American films and the Disney happy ending. Those foreign movies are hard and brutally honest but for me they also reflect the lack of optimism about the future. They present a view of the world that seems to wallow in a harsh reality that bad news is a permanent condition.

In these movies, you might see a final scene filmed in black and white where a mother is finally removing a weathered 'child missing' poster from a utility pole or community bulletin board while the camera pans out to a cold, silent street. It then moves to a dark, empty room and zooms in on toys that hadn't been used in a long time.

In the American version of this story as the mother is pulling down the poster, the scene shifts from black and white to brilliant color and we see her child come racing by on a bicycle. The camera widens out to a busy and vibrant street scene where a lot of children are playing while parents chat, and the credits begin to roll.

In real life, sadly, there've been some American outcomes more reflective of the foreign movie. But I also know that the reverse is equally true. Not all stories have a happy ending, but one of the truths about America and Americans is that we believe that we can control our own stories. It's about a deeper feeling of hope and optimism, which is so important in life. It often is the deciding factor on how your reality will turn out.

When it comes to investing, I've lost track of people that tell me to sell a stock they just bought. Such a large part of investing is self-fulfilling. Stocks go up and stocks go down and it's easy to take a loss and blame it on fate. If you're looking for the "worst case" scenario, you're likely to find it more often than not. The exact opposite is true for me. Aided by the work and knowing the history of the market, plus a natural feeling I'll be successful, has taken me very far.

Farther than anyone would've imaged when I was a teenage kid cleaning windshields at stop lights for small change.

It's my edge but it's also everyone's edge if they choose to embrace it. One could call it the American Edge.

AMERICA'S EDGE

The thing that's a far greater threat to investors, and even to America in general, is losing the optimism that tomorrow will be a better day and that opportunity never goes away. We've all seen this happen in others and it's sad. Let me illustrate what I mean.

I have a friend who wanted to break into the music business as a rapper. He was good but there are so many people with amazing talent going after a few spots. It can be the ultimate pipedream. In his mid-thirties he would talk about getting his "demo tape" out even as the industry was moving toward digital.

Over time he spoke less about renting studio time and less about "spitting knowledge" and "hot beats" and more about his rude supervisor. When he finally stopped talking about getting into the music industry and his latest verses, he became a different person. He slumped more, and he visited less frequently.

In hindsight, I feel awful for doubting him and wish I'd taken him more seriously with offers of encouragement and help. I should've gone to the studio with him sometimes and maybe found ways to help keep his dream alive. It doesn't mean he would've become a successful rapper, but he might've spent just enough time in certain circles to find other passions in the industry that could've become his destiny.

Unstoppable Prosperity brings with it the need to have unstoppable optimism and the unshakeable knowledge that you *will* get to where you want to go even if it takes a path that circles the mountain rather than a straight road to the top.

The same is true for dealing with stock market adversity.

This doesn't mean you don't have to have a strategy. It doesn't mean your portfolio won't lose value on occasion. Sometimes you might book a loss because the underlying investment proposition changed. Perhaps you needed to raise funds in order to adjust for risk in your overall portfolio.

These things happen but you cannot let them deter you from moving forward. The market always recovers and so will you.

But the more you look for the worst-case outcome from the stock market, the more likely you'll make that happen. These days there are a number of people willing to help you down that dark path. Most days, if you watch even a few minutes of financial television, you'll know fear and you'll know pessimism. The doom and gloom folks get all the air time they want.

There's no meritocracy in financial television. These permanent "bear" experts seem to get unlimited air time despite a track record of being right once in a decade or even longer. Moreover, no matter how bad eventual crashes may be, they're never as dire as the warnings would have you believe. Perhaps this is why, even when the market finally crashes, these same perma-bears routinely call for more.

"This is only the beginning" they scream like a movie villain from another galaxy looking to destroy the entire planet.

On the other hand, there are reasonable experts trying to help the viewer but, even then, your personal goals and the approach of these more positive experts might not align. After all, everyone has a specific set of goals they're trying to meet in the market.

For instance, a professional trader who is flat (has sold everything and has only cash in the account) at the end of each session or the end of each week is working from a different set of circumstances than a married couple in their forties trying to build long-term wealth.

For that couple to sell stocks to avoid a near-term pullback, correction or even a crash, with the intention of buying it back later at a lower price, or swiftly shifting to other assets like bonds, gold or the Japanese Yen, is unrealistic. Moreover, it's folly. But if their only source of information is the "bad news" pundit on television, this might be what they feel they need to do.

Then there are the experts that must always be right. They never seem to get it wrong. Today they're bullish, tomorrow bearish and always long on what's working.

I have more conviction in my own work and trust my own research to change my mind rather than what someone else is telling me I should do - and you should do the same. By using the Pillars you've learned in this book, you'll be able to take in whatever information you might learn from the television experts, filter it through your own knowledge and research and make the best decisions for your own unique situation.

Recently, there's been advice based more and more on political ideology rather than making money in the stock market. There's so much animosity about politics that these experts let it overcome their own objectivity. Be very careful of investment advice when the analyst or observer is hoping a President or company fails for personal reasons.

It might be harder to see when political ideology and disdain is the core of someone's investment advice if you feel the same way. Take care to separate your political view from your own economic future. I know lots of liberals that didn't make a penny when Ronald Reagan was President and lots of conservatives that didn't make any money in the market when Barack Obama was in the White House.

The bottom line is to be careful when you're reading about the market or watching television.

The statement to be most careful about is the line that drives me crazy: "*This isn't going to end well.*" I say to myself, "What the heck are they talking about *end*." When you know the history of the market, then you know even the worst stock market crashes in history weren't the *end* but instead they were the *beginning* of the next leg higher.

Take a look at this chart of the DOW:

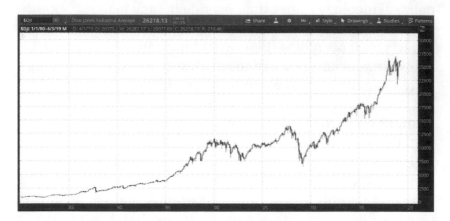

There are two major stock market crashes. One began in 2000 and the other began in 2008. Neither were "the end" unless investors joined the masses to sell stocks in great companies at terrific losses.

On the contrary, these crashes presented opportunities to get in on the ground floor, to become owners of great companies at once-in-a-lifetime bargains.

Investing isn't a baseball season that comes to an end and then starts over. But if you're smart and create a good plan, which you follow, your investments will outlive you and can go on to help your family or aid causes you care about. Investing and managing your investments must be a lifelong endeavor.

TESTING YOUR OPTIMISM

I know there'll be a rebound after the next crash and the one after that and the one after that. The market will rebound because Americans believe that tomorrow will be better than today. As long as that is the mindset of the country, the market will always recover and be stronger in that recovery.

Here's something I want you to be aware of: stock market crashes, and most corrections, often begin as an adjustment to underlying fundamentals but **always end on excessive emotions of fear and panic**. During this process, pessimism replaces optimism and for millions of Americans the door is shut on their dreams.

I get it. I've been through enough market crashes and my net worth has been hammered at times. It's gut-wrenching but there are worse feelings. When I see stocks I sold for a substantial loss, mostly out of an abundance of panic, come roaring back later I feel like crying.

In the past, I would actually take some of those stocks off my Watch List, so I didn't have to be reminded of my stupidity and pain. Later on, sometimes months or even years later, I would be watching the tape of stock symbols on my computer or television screen and a familiar symbol would scroll by with a share price that seemed inconceivable.

I'd rush to pull up a price quote and, sure enough, the stock had gone up above the price where I sold and took my loss but also above my original entry price. Then I pull up the chart, because sometimes companies with beaten down stocks do gimmicks like split the stock to make it appear more valuable.

Unfortunately, for me that's hardly ever the case. The simple fact is the stock has come charging back, making the kind of move higher that wouldn't have surprised me when I initially thought it was worth owning. But I sold, which might've been prudent. But the real mistake was taking my eye off the stock and erasing it from my screen out of anger or shame.

If I would've continued to monitor the stock there would've been chances to see things like price movement, stock breakouts, spikes in volume and news alerts that might've lured me back into the stock. Instead I sulked, and I missed the rebound.

So, there is a lesson here. When you close a position, it's important to put the stock back on your Watch List. From time to time come back and monitor the progress of the stock. It might not come back to a point where you want to buy again, but you have the option and can take advantage if the stock begins to rebound. It's a small investment of time for a potentially big profit.

You're going to invest time to know companies so don't let this valuable time go to waste. Once you close a position, whether for profit or loss, keep it on your Watch List so you can check it out occasionally because all companies evolve.

When you simply walk away from the market after a bruising experience, you're giving up on your "demo tapes" of dreams. You begin seeing the world through a foreboding black and white lens of the future that accepts a worst-case possibility as the ultimate reality.

I'm not interested in terms like **bull** and **bear** market. When things are going great and the market is on auto-pilot, it doesn't need a term. And when it's in freefall, there are lots of terms said privately that are a lot harsher than "bear market" or "correction." I don't get hung up on terminology and I don't want you to either. Many investors believe that you make money in a bull market and lose money in a bear market. I believe you should make money in any market. It doesn't matter what label it carries. The ability to make money regardless of what the market is doing is how you obtain Unstoppable Prosperity. It's why I wrote this book and why you're reading it.

There's no doubt broad market moves provide cover for lots of stocks to rally higher than their investment proposition would indicate. Market meltdowns hit all stocks, even those of wonderful companies doing everything right. But the aftermath of stock market crashes doesn't last long in the grand scheme of things.

HISTORIC LESSONS FROM CRASHES AND BEAR MARKETS

Since I graduated from high school in 1980, there've been four stock market crashes and they all have the same things in common. They've been short-lived, but they hurt like hell.

Bear Market Period	Duration	Decline
Nov 1980 to Aug 1982	21 months	-27.8%
Aug 1987 to Dec 1987	4 month	-33.5%
Mar 2000 to Oct 2000	7 months	-49.1%
Oct 2007 to Mar 2009	17 months	-56.4%

These "bear markets" have been followed by recoveries that eventually saw the market hit new, all-time highs. It wasn't always that way. For instance, the most infamous of all stock market crashes, the Crash of 1929, took 25 years to get back to breakeven.

Dow Jones Industrial Average

Sep 3, 1929 – 381.17

Nov 23, 1954 – 382.0

So why did it appear to take so long for the market to recover? Well, that 25-year period is a little misleading. When adjusted for deflation and the fact that IBM was taken out of the index in 1939 (the stock wasn't reinstated until 1979) and the fact that it went on to significantly outperform plus provide dividend payments, the adjusted numbers would've seen investors get back to breakeven in *less than five years*. In 1932, the Dow Jones paid an average 14% dividend yield.

So, after the worst economic crash in the history of the world, the market would've recovered in just 5 years. That's resiliency by anyone's standards.

NIFTY FIFTY

I began my career on Wall Street as an entry level analyst at EF Hutton reviewing trades made by several desks, including the bond desk. My job gave me exposure to all aspects of the business where I was able to ask lots of questions.

Moreover, I was able to learn from folks that lived through crashes, bear markets, evolving market truisms and conventional wisdom. Back in 1985, the demise of the so-called "Nifty Fifty" was still talked about all the time as a cautionary tale. It wasn't about crazy speculation, like the Tulip Mania in the 1600s or even wild enthusiasm about a "new paradigm" with technology stocks in the late 1990s.

The Nifty Fifty bubble was about owning great stocks without regard for valuations. The rally in these stocks was based on the premise that the stocks had to be owned and were "great at any price" to hold indefinitely.

Looking back, it's easy to understand the excitement of the times. The 1960s was a decade of progress in technology. It was the beginning of the computer age and a decade that allowed mankind to "touch the face of God" with space programs that broke the bonds of earth's gravitational pull.

The nation felt invincible and these stocks were the best representatives. They couldn't be beaten, and they were safe. Some even called them "widow and orphan" stocks because of the perception that they were too big to fail. In reality, a few did fail but many became a poor risk in terms of valuation.

Many of the names that drove the Nifty Fifty of the 1960s are still important publicly traded companies:

Anheuser-Busch
Bristol-Myers
Coca-Cola Company
Dow Chemical
Eli Lilly and Company
General Electric
IBM
International Flavors and Fragrances
Johnson & Johnson
Minnesota Mining and Manufacturing (3M)
McDonald's
Merck & Co.
MGIC Investment Corporation
PepsiCo
Pfizer
Philip Morris Cos.
Procter & Gamble
Schlumberger
Texas Instruments
The Walt Disney Company
Walmart
Xerox

But other Nifty Fifty names are no longer publicly traded having merged with other companies or business declined too greatly to be listed:

American Home Products
AMP Inc.
Avon Products
Baxter International
Black & Decker
Burroughs Corporation
Chesebrough-Ponds
Eastman Kodak
Digital Equipment Corporation
Emery Air Freight
First National City Bank
Gillette
International Telephone and Telegraph
Louisiana Land & Exploration
Lubrizol
Polaroid
Revlon
Schering Plough
Joseph Schlitz Brewing Company
Sears, Roebuck and Company
Simplicity Pattern
Squibb
S.S. Kresge
Upjohn

The moral of the story is that when the dust settles some stocks are great to buy and hold indefinitely if the value proposition is in place. But even the greatest companies in the world can have stocks that are too expensive. Let's look at some specifics.

Price to Earnings (PE) Ratio in 1972

- S&P 500 = 19
- Nifty Fifty = 42

Like so many other market swoons, it wasn't the weight of overvaluation that triggered the selloff but a dark shadow that descended over the nation. In the case of the Nifty Fifty, the early 1970s was a decided "downer" for the nation:

- Vietnam War came into our living room and we were losing
- Watergate Controversy
- Arab Oil Embargo
- Massive Inflation
- Americans Turning On, Tuning In and Dropping Out
- College Campus Unrest
- Pollution Crisis
- Crime Crisis

Soon invincibility gave way to rampant insecurity. A more vulnerable nation was reflected in a stock market where great stocks were simply too expensive, like Disney changing hands at PE ratios of 82 and McDonalds at 86.

At some point, "growth at any price" stops working - often when stocks are so lofty in valuations that they come down very rapidly.

Creative destruction means even the largest companies will be vulnerable to increased competition at some point, even those considered industry monopolies.

TIMELESS PORTFOLIO MAKE-UP

As an investor, these events will recur over and over and underscore why the ultimate portfolio should include:

- Short-term trading positions
- Intermediate-term buy and hold positions
- Long-term core holdings

There are several actions investors should consider when the market is in trouble, including:

- Holding core positions in great companies
- Taking losses on companies where the value proposition changed
- Holding Cash
- Holding boring, high dividend-paying stocks
- Acquiring old, boring, high dividend-paying stocks

In an investment world where everyone is chasing performance and trying to beat the market daily, the number of winners becomes narrower. Rallies create more buyers who push share prices higher. This, in turn, lures additional buyers.

This cycle is the challenge of passive investing, which is the approach of many money managers. This may work fine on the way up but exacerbates the move on the way down. It's one of the reasons I feel so strongly about you being in charge of your own investments.

Lost in all the excitement over hot stocks in recent years (in past years too) are those old names that've been around long enough to have adjusted business models to modern times. In 2018, those names did very well while many of the "high-fliers" were grounded.

Interestingly, some of the same Nifty Fifty names that were overvalued a few decades ago are now changing hands at below broad market valuations. This chart shows the 2018 total return for these stocks (which includes the increase in share value and dividend payouts).

Company Stock Symbol	Year Established	2018 Total Return
Eli Lilly (LLY)	1876	40.4%
Merck (MRK)	1891	40.0%
Church & Dwight (CHD)	1846	33.2%
Macy's (M)	1858	23.7%
Hormel (HRL)	1891	19.7%
McCormick (MKC)	1889	39.0%
Pfizer (PFE)	1849	25.3%

CASH IS KING

When the market is in a steep decline and it's time to make big decisions, the biggest decision is when to take a loss. Fighting against the thought of not only losing money but losing money on an idea you once thought would be a major winner can be a tough pill to swallow. And the urge to pick the bottom is a temptation even seasoned investors can find hard to resist.

In those instances, investors should embrace the notion of holding as much cash as possible to put to work at some point. Like holding onto boring dividend stocks, an investor can often get paid to wait while holding cash, depending on where interest rates are.

There have been periods when cash made huge returns:

1998	5.1%
1999	4.7%
2000	6.0%
2001	4.1%
2006	4.8%
2007	4.7%

In 2018, the return was 1.8%, which was enough to be the best performing asset class of the year.

Cash (money markets)	+1.8%
U.S. Bonds	+0.2%
U.S. Corp Bonds	-1.5%
Gold	-2.6%
S&P 500	-6.2%
U.S. Real Estate	-8.3%
U.S. Small Caps	-13.0%
Commodities	-13.9%
Emerging Markets	-16.9%
Crude	-24.8%

When you see the market in a significant downturn you must make some adjustments, including raising cash. It's unrealistic, and a serious mistake, to think you're going to hop in and out of assets that are working. Forget about the notion that there's a bull market somewhere at any time and you could be in that bull market. It's not going to happen. Moreover, it's a giant mistake for an investor, with the goal of building wealth, to play that game.

But wild gyrations in the market do offer great opportunities for **short-term trades**. In an ideal portfolio, 15% should be used for trades based on a list of stocks you know want to go higher.

My same Three Pillars apply to these short-term ideas, but the weightings change in the decision-making process.

70% Technical

20% Fundamental

10% Behavioral

REMAINING DISCIPLINED WHEN CLOSING POSITIONS

This can be the hard part, especially when you're taking a loss. It can be even harder if it means taking a loss on a stock that, at one point, was a winner.

People rarely ask me about closing a stock, which is amazing. It reveals that most investors don't have a game plan for the entire life cycle of an investment.

Generally, when it's a question of taking profits, I usually respond that they should take profits the same way they would take a loss. But this can present its own set of problems as well.

I believe you should use the same rationale to exit a position that you used to enter the investment. In other words, if you plan to trade a stock after holding it for a few days, you should not hold it longer just because of an exaggerated move either higher or lower, but especially lower. That can be easier said than done, however. Remember to avoid emotions when investing. Overcome the urge to "hang on just a bit longer to see what's going to happen."

This should apply when employing my research steps as well. If you're satisfied with using earnings trends and charts as buy signals, then you should use them as sell signals as well. If these steps are just the start of the research process, as it is for me with my longer-term positions, then major changes must be noted, and a greater sense of urgency added to reevaluate fundamentals.

Case Study

On September 25, 2018, Amazon posted its financial results after the close of trading. The earnings were a monster "beat", coming in at $5.75 per share against a Wall Street consensus of $3.14. However, the rest of the report was troublesome.

1. Revenue at $56.6 billion missed consensus of $57.1 billion
2. AWS (cloud) revenue at $6.68 billion missed consensus estimates of $6.71 billion
3. Guidance was a huge disappointment

When the stock opened the next day, it was pure carnage. Plunging at one point by more than 10% (its worst decline since January 2014). The stock, which began the week changing hands at $1,789 a share, finished Friday, October 26 at $1,642 a share.

FUNDAMENTAL SELL SIGNAL

The day before Amazon posted the bombshell earnings report that knocked the juggernaut off course, and to its worst session in several years, the earnings consensus for both fiscal years 2018 and 2019 came down sharply.

EPS Trend	FY 2018	FY 2019
Oct 24, 2018	17.32	25.12
Oct 3, 2018	**17.50**	**25.64**
Aug 29, 2018	17.35	25.37
Aug 1, 2018	17.13	25.10

Disciplined short-term investors should have closed the stock at that very moment, no questions asked. When a stock is on autopilot and in constant rally mode, short-term investors should worry when earnings estimates are unchanged for a couple of weeks.

In this case, with a juggernaut stock that was already looking weaker than normal, the decline was a true sell signal.

TECHNICAL SELL SIGNAL

Another important marker could be found in the technical chart, for those who were looking. Amazon shares were going up every single session, so much so that any down session would stand out. The trendline was perfect, holding through most of 2018. On October 5th the stock failed to hold the trendline sending out a red flag.

Coupled with the double top formation, this was a 100% sell signal for any short-term investors more concerned with near-term momentum and technical factors. That would've meant closing the stock around $1,950 a share and avoiding a lot of near-term pain.

2018 MELT DOWN

There were a lot of contributing factors to the market meltdown of 2018, including non-stop negative speculation about the market and the economy.

It all began in late January when the 10-Year U.S. Treasury yield began to edge higher, closer to 3.0%.

Then, on February 2nd the Bureau of Labor released its monthly jobs report. The report was great but for Wall Street it seemed too great because wages climbed 2.9% year over year. This sent stocks into a tailspin. Speculation ran rampant that this positive report would be enough to unleash the Federal Reserve.

The crazy thing about the freak-out that saw the Dow Jones Industrial Average drop 666 points was that three percent yields on the 10-Year U.S. Treasury Bond have never been associated with market tops even though this market seemed to be reacting as if it was.

Rates have generally been much higher than 3.0% ahead of market corrections and the onset of recessions. The history is pretty clear:

Market Peaks and Bond Yields			
Period	Loss	10-Year Yield	Rate Trend
Nov 1980 - Aug 1982	-27.80%	12.40%	Higher
Aug 1987 - Dec 1987	-33.50%	8.7%	higher
Mar 2000 - Oct 2000	-49.10%	6.20%	Lower
Oct 2007 - Mar 2009	-56.40%	4.50%	Lower

GUESSING TOPS = CREATING TOPS

Sometimes the chattering class can scream so much and so often they finally spook the market.

The key word of 2018 among many observers was "peak," as in, "It doesn't get better than this." The implication was that things would be getting decidedly worse.

On April 24th the CFO of Caterpillar remarked during the first quarter earnings conference call that results were great, but it might have been the "high water" mark. This comment sent the stock, and the broad market, spiraling.

After that virtually every bit of good news, whether corporate or economic, was greeted with the assumption that it simply couldn't get any better. Bad news was just around the corner.

This created an environment where bad news was bad news and good news was bad news. Even in this environment the market still found an even keel and rallied to new highs.

However, the tone was set for the actual knockout blow. This came in the form of comments from the Federal Reserve suggesting very aggressive action to slow the economy. This was to include removal of billions of dollars of liquidity each month, regardless of economic conditions and data. That was on October 3, 2018.

The S&P 500 proceeded to smash under a trendline that had been in place for close to three years:

BANDWAGON TIP OVER

For years, Wall Street has "dissed" individual investors as being the perfect foils and easy marks when it comes to stock market tops. While there's some truth to the idea that investors can become too optimistic as a herd, this isn't the exclusive distinction for individual investors.

The "smartest guys in the room" rarely seem to have unique ideas and like to gather together with similar stock ratings and broad market calls.

2017 was winding down from what, arguably, could be considered the best market year ever, considering overall gains, lack of volatility and very few down days. Every session felt like an idyllic summer day with the perfect temperature and breeze.

Wall Street firms were asked for their thoughts on 2018 and they all saw wonderful blue skies ahead.

Firm	2018 S&P 500 Target
Bank of America	2,800
Bank of Montreal	2,950
Canaccord	2,800
Citigroup	2,675
Credit Suisse	2,875
Deutsche Bank	2,850
Evercore ISI	3,000
Goldman Sachs	2,850
HSBC	2,650
Jefferies	2,855
Morgan Stanley	2,750
Scotiabank	2,750
Stifel Nicolaus	2,750
UBS	2,900
Median	2,825

Source: Fortune

As it turned out, it was a good year, until it wasn't. Wall Street missed the mark by a mile. The consensus of firms in the table above saw 2018 S&P 500 finishing the year at 2,819 but the index closed the year at 2,506, the worst of the big three indices.

Dow Jones Industrial Average

+25.1% 2017

-5.6% 2018

NASDAQ Composite

+28.2% 2017

-4.0% 2018

S&P 500

+19.4% 2017

-6.2% 2018

Understanding the Wall Street herd mentality is part of our behavioral approach and important to know. A great research piece from FactSet.com reveals some interesting insights.

They grouped all publicly traded stocks into five quintiles. From left to right, the most "buy" recommendations at the start of the year to the last quintile on the right which had the fewest "buy" ratings coming into 2018.

Their study showed that the stocks with the fewest buy ratings as a percentage of overall analysts' coverage had the best performance in 2018.

Conversely, those stocks where everyone was on the bandwagon finished the year with the worst performance. This is remarkable and confirms investor hunches and gives them greater belief they should find an alternative rather than blindly following Wall Street analysts.

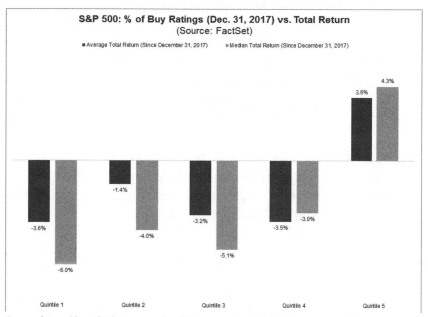

Source: https://insight.factset.com/sp-500-companies-with-lowest-percent-of-buy-ratings-are-top-performers-in-2018

What you must understand as an investor is that when everyone has a "buy rating" on a stock the next rating has to be a downgrade. This is true for the downside as well. If a stock has a "sell rating" across the board, the next ratings change can only be positive from there.

When assessing overall market risk, know that an overly bullish Wall Street is a yellow flag. Instead of adding to your confidence, it should get you to review your portfolio and assess which names might have to be closed in the event the market turns south.

NOW YOU KNOW

If you're in the market long enough, you'll be "lucky" enough to deal with several market corrections along with three or four crashes and subsequent recoveries. These inevitable events shouldn't stop you from investing. On the contrary, you should be taking advantage of these moments in time. I'm not saying try to pick exact bottoms, but I am saying the oldest axiom in investing is *buy low, sell high*.

For those that are less inclined to do the work, regular investing, which includes dollar cost averaging, will allow you to pick the bottom, although it'll leave you defenseless to mitigate the damage of market meltdowns.

Of course, I believe in doing the work and getting the most out of each investment dollar. These days when the market goes haywire and begins to plunge, I get very excited. If it's happening on non-fundamental news, I become outright giddy.

Ultimately, you must be optimistic and knowledgeable about all facets of the market to avoid mistakes and maximize opportunities.

NOW EXECUTE

We know that corrections, pullbacks and even crashes are part of the market and will impact all investors at some time. For the uninformed, these market dips and swoons often come as a surprise, which shouldn't be the case but too often is.

We can use a bit of recent history to help us learn and make sure we have a plan to handle these events. I want you to go back to the end of 2018 when the market took that serious dip that had everybody talking for days. There are two things I want you to do with that information using several stocks from your own portfolio.

If you aren't in the market yet pick several popular stocks or stocks that you've been watching. Treat them as if you had them in your portfolio.

1. Go back one month before the downturn and see if you can locate the warning signs that something might be on the way. Look at both the stocks themselves and the larger economic news. I've given you some of the indicators in this chapter, but you'll probably find others that were there.

2. Then, using two or three of your own stocks determine what would've happened if you would've sold the stocks one week before the downturn and then bought back in on February 15, 2019. Would you have made or lost money? It will vary from stock to stock and there's no absolute answer. Where would you be if you held the stock through the downturn? Again, there's no right answer, but there's learning to be accomplished here.

Being optimistic doesn't mean hanging on blindly to positions at all times. It does mean you have the belief, as I do, that the market will ALWAYS recover and recover more quickly than the doomsayers would have you believe. It does mean that you look at things practically, using your knowledge of the fundamental values of your portfolio and a clear goal for each position in that portfolio. After more than three decades in the market, I believe more than ever that the stock market is the greatest creator of wealth ever devised. I want you to have your share of that wealth, to have Unstoppable Prosperity.

CHAPTER SEVEN

ROOKIE MISTAKES EVEN
EXPERIENCED TRADERS MAKE

Nobody's perfect. Everybody misses on occasional trades or investments from time to time. But through this book I've shown you ways to minimize those misses. I've always said, "The next best thing to making money is NOT LOSING too much money."

Yet, I constantly see both experienced investors and novices making mistakes that can be easily avoided. We've discussed the big issues of portfolio management and how to best manage and even profit from those downturns that are part of every market cycle. Now, I want to address some of the more common, obvious mistakes that investors and traders make all too often.

I want you to come back to this chapter regularly, until you're totally comfortable with this information. I want you to be able to "catch yourself" before you make any of these mistakes. I've said repeatedly that mistakes are part of being in the market and each time you make one you're fine - AS LONG AS YOU LEARN FROM IT!

And never let them stop you from your long-term investment goals.

There are some mistakes that we can avoid without having to go through the "hard knocks" learning process. After all, self-sabotage is the greatest enemy investors face in the stock market.

A quick and very positive note before we move on to the mistakes, there's great news! The costs to enter and exit investments are becoming cheaper and cheaper. When I started on Wall Street, a "roundtrip" buying and selling of a stock could cost investors as much as $1,000. However, while the cost of an individual transaction has dropped dramatically, the lessons remain expensive for those taking the plunge without a proper game plan.

We've discussed the need for a strategy throughout this book. Whenever you take on a new position, whether with the intention of short-term trading or long-term buy and hold, you *must* have a plan for that position. You need to make sure the ease and inexpensive nature of investing today doesn't create a false sense of security and lull you into an approach that doesn't include all of the research we've discussed throughout this book. Inexpensive trades don't make up for poor choices. Poor choices make any trade an expensive proposition.

CLASSIC MISTAKES

Investors, both old and new, make mistakes but newer investors make them much more frequently.

This occurs because they haven't observed the market's actions and patterns over a long enough period of time to learn the "truths" that time reveals.

Let's take a look at some of the most common, and most destructive, mistakes investors make and how you can avoid them:

1. Buying "cheap" stocks
2. Selling too soon
3. Hanging on to losers too long
4. Buying overhyped stocks
5. Gaming and blaming market dips
6. Buying only one stock
7. Letting the news get you down

MISTAKE #1 - BUYING "CHEAP" STOCKS

Believe me, I get it. We all want to be stock moguls. Owning tens of thousands of shares of stock makes investors feel great. The stock price doesn't have to move a lot for a major financial windfall if you're holding a great number of shares. The problem is that judging a stock simply on share price relegates investors to buying the riskiest stocks in the market. Ironically, this quite often destructively dovetails with the "buying only one stock" mistake, I'll discuss shortly.

It's been my experience that most stocks changing hands under $10 per share represent broken companies with enormous problems or unproven companies with significant hurdles they've yet to overcome.

That's just the way it is and has been for quite a long time. Think of this as the "bargain bin," where you can get things cheaply but there's probably a reason for that lower price. On the other end of the price spectrum, I find that stocks with share prices trading above $100 per share are more often than not, actually "cheap".

What I find after thoroughly researching both lower and higher-priced stocks, and considering their current stock price, is that most of the so-called "cheaper stocks" are not a bargain. Moreover, stocks labeled as expensive due to high shares prices, even those over $1,000 per share, are often extremely undervalued (with respect to the earnings and growth they're delivering). That's why professionals are willing to pay such a "high" share price for them! It's not the actual price they're focusing on but rather the value **at that price** that each share represents.

For a moment, try to forget about the number of shares and focus on the return on your investment:

If you have $1,600 to invest you could buy;

> 1,000 shares of $1.60 stock
>
> 10 shares of a $160.00 stock
>
> 1 share of a $1,600 stock

People always ask me, rather incredulously, "How can I make money with one or two shares of stock?" That's really not a bad question. My answer would be two words, "Grand Slams." Let me give you some examples.

Grand Slams

In 2012 there was an article on seven stocks, which were changing hands at $500 per share or more.

Stock Symbol	Company Name	Mar 2012 Share Price	Number of Shares
ISRG	Intuitive Surgical	$529	3
AAPL	Apple Inc.	$602	2
GOOG	Google LLC.	$634	2
PCLN	Priceline Group	$697	2
NVR	NVR Inc.	$741	2
SEB	Seaboard Corporation	$1,955	1
BRKA	Berkshire Hathaway Inc. Class A	$122,115	1

If you had $1,600 and bought any of the stocks priced below $1,000 per share on this list, you'd be so much better off than having not invested at all or limiting the stocks you own to only those changing hands at much lower prices.

Using my Three Pillars I've taught you throughout this book, you would've seen that any of these stocks would have been a solid investment. You could've timed your trades to maximize your return. Just glancing at the share prices in 2012 scared off many investors before they even took the time to do a quick look. That isn't a mistake you should make knowing what you do now.

Furthermore, it's hard to imagine that investors could've found any seven stocks in 2012 that outperformed this list. Sadly, so many investors didn't buy them because they "cost too much."

That has to stop NOW!

Look at the percentage returns on those 5 of the 7 that you could have purchased with your $1,600 investment. There were two stocks on that list that cost more than that and if you had purchased even one share the return would've been remarkable.

One share of SEB at $1,955 would be worth $3,684 or 88% more!

One share of BRK.A at $122,115 would be worth $315,800 or 159% more!

Also, note the fact that these returns on investment were achieved in just a few years!

Stock Symbol	Company Name	Mar 2012 Share Price	Number of Shares	Current Value	% Return
ISRG	Intuitive Surgical	$529	3	$5,040	217.58%
AAPL	Apple Inc.	$602	2	$3,178	163.95%
GOOG	Google LLC.	$634	2	$2,436	92.11%
PCLN	Priceline Group	$697	2	$3,902	179.91%
NVR	NVR Inc.	$741	2	$5,336	260.05%
SEB	Seaboard Corporation	$1,955	1	$3,684	88.44%
BRKA	Berkshire Hathaway Inc. Class A	$122,115	1	$315,800	158.61%

Note: *ISRG shares were split 3 to 1 on October 6, 2017 and Apple shares were split 7 to 1 on June 9, 2014, just to be clear with respect to the prices noted in the table.*

To understand how powerful the returns have been for those "expensive" stocks, consider that even at a 10% compounded growth on $1,600 your return during that same time period would've been $2,834. Each stock's performance surpasses that value by a significant margin. Of course, it's been a long time since any bank has paid out 10% interest, which is another thing we must not forget.

I know it's counterintuitive that a stock with a low share price isn't automatically cheap and, in fact, might be expensive. Throughout the book I've shown you how to discern value and to identify high-quality opportunities. By now you understand that the price of a stock that is underperforming is a much greater expense to your goal of Unstoppable Prosperity than an overachieving stock that has a higher price tag. The solution to this mistake is that you have to accept that the idea of "cheap" and "expensive" that might exist outside of your investments doesn't necessarily work for your portfolio.

Get Used to Buying "Expensive" Stocks.

Considering comments from management, it seems unlikely Apple shares will split anymore, which means potential investors have to get over the "high" share price and focus on the value that each share represents.

Generally, stock splits are seen as a gimmick to lure individual investors and do nothing to add economic value for shareholders. You must get used to buying stocks that are changing hands in the hundred dollar per share range or even in the thousands of dollars per share range.

Realize that the hottest publicly traded companies don't care if individual investors own their stock. They prefer that institutions own the stock. That's right, they want you to use their products, but you aren't invited to join their fortune-making party. They assume you'll be intimidated by an "expensive" share price.

Let's crash that party!

We're going to use the products and tell our friends how great the products are, not only because we like the products, but also because we're part owners of the company making the products. That's how we get our piece of the action. That's how we get Unstoppable Prosperity.

MISTAKE #2 - SELLING TOO SOON

I want to make a quick distinction here. If the purpose of any holding is for a short-term profit and you see that profit realized, then **act on your plan** and move out of that stock. You can use trailing stops to let those positions ride, but those stops must be adjusted higher as the shares move higher. If you're unfamiliar with trailing stops let me give you a quick explanation. A trailing stop is an order to sell the stock if it begins to drop - either to a certain price or by a specific percentage.

By the same token, those 'trading' positions, bought with the intent of a quick trade, must also apply to taking a loss. If you intend to take a quick profit and the stock trends downward, you need to exit the position. Unfortunately, some traders will continue to hang on, waiting for the stock to rebound, resulting in even greater losses.

If you've done your homework and have found a solid company with real growth potential, jumping out of that position when the stock ticks up slightly can be a real mistake and belies your goals and game plan of achieving Unstoppable Prosperity. We've discussed how much of your portfolio should be in long-term investments and how much should be in short-term trading. Stick with your plan!

Many factors contribute to this mistake, but it boils down to good old-fashioned human nature. We're anxious when it comes to taking risks and more so when we have no idea what we're doing. When we do this repeatedly, we go from bad investment habits to pure financial sabotage.

The mistake of selling a stock for small gains when we bought with the intent of holding is the result of a lack of faith in the stocks we own. This is especially true in the face of broader stock market weakness or volatility.

Let's dive in first on selling too soon for small gains.

Consider this situation. You've completed your quick analysis and the deeper dive into the fundamentals (which I'll talk about in Chapter 8) of a company and have identified a solid investment opportunity. Then you've invested the time to analyze the charts and found a good time to initiate your investment in a stock. Why jump out after you're up a few bucks?

To arrive at the point you did, and to have pulled the trigger on the trade, required time, effort and energy. You didn't engage in all that to only make a few dollars. That wasn't your plan. Your plan was to truly invest in a company with a stock price that had serious upside potential. A small pop higher in price isn't "serious" potential but rather quick profits.

Trading is about quick profits, but investing is about bigger dollars and wealth building. If you analyzed a company and planned to be an investor in the company, a few dollars higher does not a successful investor make!

The problem for most newer investors at that point is that they lack perspective. That causes them to be nervous and to not want to "give back" their paper profits. That's just human nature doing its thing. Trust me, I get that. I had to overcome that fear of mismanaging a "winner" into a "loser" a long time ago, but I've never forgotten that concern. It's only natural.

Here's what worked for me.

Go back and take a look at stock charts of good companies, the kind you believe you'll invest in. You'll see that trends in prices of good companies last far longer and push much further than most people would ever imagine.

That's what did it for me. I realized that by opting for that quick and satisfying small profit (succumbing to natural fears), I was dramatically hurting my chances to build serious wealth, which, of course, was my main goal!

That will help cure you fairly quickly! We must maintain the proper perspective at all times. It's not always easy, but it's something we must strive for, even when the markets are acting irrationally - which we know they will from time to time! It's not always smooth sailing! If you apply my Three Pillars when making investing decisions, you'll have the knowledge and confidence to stick with the winners rather than giving in to human nature and opt for the quick, small profit. Moreover, the decision to close an investment position will be based mostly on fundamentals.

MISTAKE #3 - HANGING ON TO LOSERS TOO LONG

There's a vicious behavioral "two-headed" monster that we all battle. We've just confronted the first "head" - *selling too soon*. The other "head" of the monster is *hanging on to losers too long*, and I learned my lesson on this front a long time ago as well. But learn it I did!

I understand this one too well: you've done all the work, you're ready to go, the market just needs to cooperate. Now, here's the thing that makes everything messy, YOUR analysis is on the line. And since that's the case, on some level, YOUR EGO is now involved. When ego becomes involved, it can create emotional rough spells that become financial disasters, if we aren't careful.

To be sure, there are psychological rewards when you make money on a stock you purchased based on your own reasoning. That's how it's supposed to work!

It's great to celebrate winners, but only for a moment. It's really important to limit that emotional pendulum. We need to be clear-headed if the stock starts going the other way and be prepared to act. Emotional balance is necessary for successful investing.

While it feels great making money in the stock market, it feels so much worse losing money. There've been numerous psychological studies that all conclude people take an emotional hit from losing money that's exponentially greater than the joy of making money.

It's even more difficult losing in the stock market than, say, a slot machine in Las Vegas. When it comes to the stock market, there's an intellectual element. Everyone wants to be thought of as a smart investor. So, we feel "dumb" when we lose money.

Nobody wants to feel dumb. That's why it's critical that you do your homework and truly understand the fundamentals of every company in which you invest. AND you MUST make decisions that are based on facts, not emotions. Hanging on to a stock that's turned down and is a loser just because it would hurt to "feel dumb" just compounds a bad situation. This has to be avoided.

Not all our ideas will instantly be winners. In fact, there'll be times when more sellers than buyers send a stock much lower than would seem appropriate, based on the research you did.

Maybe we missed something and should go back to the drawing board.

Maybe the market is right, and we simply got it wrong.

You must reconcile this with an honest assessment of your work. On one hand we're going to make our fortune, in part by relying on proven research techniques, which means ignoring the emotions of the crowds.

If the work is right and if your research is comprehensive and accurate, you can add to the position, or "double down." This also means that you must be prepared to take losses if you choose to add to the position. **Adding to a "losing" position is one of the greatest risks you can take**. Depending on how much money you have in the market, I mostly recommend against it.

I've seen people add to positions ostensibly to lower their cost again and again. They buy a stock at $50 and add more at $45 which brings their average cost to $47.50. It's simply not worth taking money out of your cash pile, or from other potential ideas, to add to one that is moving in the wrong direction. This becomes more like aggressive gambling rather than smart investing.

Investing Lesson: for those that do add to a position, don't merge the two entry costs into an average price because this will negatively impact your ability to make a smart exit if that becomes necessary.

Case in point:

> You buy XYZ at $100
>
> You add XYZ at $50
>
> Average costs $75

A few months after the second buy of XYZ the stock rallies to $70 a share but starts to lose momentum. Major firms begin adjusting their earnings estimates lower as well as their ratings on the stock.

But you don't close the position because you're not at the breakeven point of $75.00. That's nuts! It would be a good chance to close the entire position and at the very least you take profits on the second purchase. Closing that second purchase at $70 means a 40% profit and more cash to put to work elsewhere. By averaging the two buys, you disguise the potential profits from the second buy.

I guarantee there'll be times when a stock moves against you and that move will be quickly confirmed by your research, but you'll be tempted to hold on.

Maybe you could point to a stock you owned years ago but sold for a loss and that stock eventually turned around to become a winner. Just as there are positions we buy with the intent of short-term trading, there could be a position or two we own for its very long-term potential, but we make that distinction **before** we buy not after. If we do it after, we're rationalizing reasons to hold which is the result of our emotions and ego impacting our thinking.

Compounding the emotional tug of war would be to add to losing positions. I call this the "Captain Ahab Syndrome."

The specter of taking a big loss becomes Moby Dick and the madness of avoiding the loss means putting more money at risk until you threaten to destroy everything. Protecting your ego can be a very expensive proposition. In fact, the biggest losses I've ever seen came from the smartest people protecting their egos rather than protecting their portfolios.

I've seen doctors lose fortunes in medical stocks and engineers lose fortunes in technology stocks. It's great to have a head start based on professional knowledge but you must be able to measure it against reality.

The discipline that my Three Pillars provide help avoid this insidious trap.

MISTAKE #4 - BUYING OVERHYPED STOCKS

Let's first consider a question:

By the time the media has reached a fevered pitch in discussing a particular company or industry, is it likely we're too late to the party?

Every situation is somewhat unique, but my answer would be: *Probably*.

These days, there's a race for eyeballs that is rapidly changing the power center of media and putting more pressure on sensationalism and clickbait rather than in-depth reporting. Making matters more difficult for investors is the reality that while there are more media sources than ever, actual information beyond headlines is scarce.

Moreover, ideology and caution seem to play an ever-greater role in interpreting news. This can result in a "doom and gloom" interpretation of the day's events in the market by media outlets.

I understand this concern. The biggest financial media outlets seemed to cheerlead Americans over the financial cliff when the market crashed in 2001. As a result, today the over exuberance is reserved for the hottest sector of the moment, often before the fundamentals match the hype.

For those same reasons, the media often feels the need to pour cold water on positive news or make predictions about the next worst-case scenario. These negative guesses become the lead and dominate the narrative. I watch folks on financial television successfully talk down individual stocks, and the entire market, all the time.

If you aren't armed with knowledge that comes from your own assessment of the actual sources, you can get swept up and make costly mistakes. Forget the headlines and the knee jerk reactions to all the information out there. You owe it to yourself to check out the information you use, so you can properly filter misinformation.

Going to the source and seeing the information yourself is also very liberating and will help you build your confidence as you gain more and more experience with your investments.

Best Sources:

- The company's website and historic SEC filings
- Conference call transcripts
- Industry periodicals and websites (unbiased evaluations on products and trends)
- Local Media (Many times I've learned more from employees complaining to local media than SEC filings)
- Wall Street research reports
- News media interviews: YouTube and podcasts

If you find yourself leaning in a certain direction based on personal angst or worry, you'll naturally seek out additional voices. That's a natural reaction to crisis. But listening to "experts" who don't know your personal situation, who don't have your goals as their primary focus, can result in you making decisions that are counter to your best interests. When you have doubts or worries be sure to go back to my Pillars. Focus on doing the work yourself. That's why you went through the process in the first place.

Sometimes investors go looking for someone to corroborate a hunch or an investment they've already made. It's a nice way to mask mistakes and self-inflicted wounds. This may feel good at the moment but it's just a way to assuage their egos and it's still a formula for losing money. If you want your mistakes and anger validated, then channel surf for a bit and someone will say something that makes you feel better. But that doesn't make you money. I'm not saying that you shouldn't be aware of financial news. I'm saying that you need to be a critical consumer of that news, both good and bad. Nothing can replace your own research and efforts when it's time to make decisions.

MISTAKE #5 - GAMING AND BLAMING MARKET DIPS

We know the market goes down from time to time and even the greatest stocks have periods when share price is correcting (down 10%) or even moves into bear territory (down 20%). Many investors have convinced themselves they can game these dips.

It's a huge mistake for any investor, or would-be investor, to wait around for a stock to pullback in the hopes of getting the stock at a cheaper price. When I hear this, I know that it's just a tacit admission of what they perceive as a mistake. They didn't buy the stock at a lower price and don't want to look foolish buying it now when it's trading higher.

Yes, we're back to dealing with personal psychology and the need to avoid looking or feeling dumb. Talk about making investing more like gambling! The notion that a great stock is going to pull all the way back to a share price you wish you'd taken when you had the chance but hesitated is folly. Worse, it's just compounding the mistake.

Now you don't want to be a chump, that person the experts excoriate on television all day long for "chasing" stocks. No one wants to feel like they're being taken advantage of in any situation. You certainly don't want to be "chasing" the stock just because the price is going up. However, you are going to be a chump *if* you know a stock is a great investment at its current share price and don't act on your knowledge.

Because I've been in the market for as long as I have, I can let you in on a secret that the "experts" would rather you never know. Often, they're either "chasing" those same stocks to make money or have missed incredible money-making opportunities for the same rookie mistake of waiting for the dip.

The classic example of this is the market swoon during the Great Recession that saw the market bottom in March 2009. Back then, virtually every expert that went on television told investors there was more pain to come. They were convinced that the initial market rebound should be ignored because the lows would be re-tested.

The market never re-tested the lows and millions of individual investors are still waiting. Now they're in a deeper conundrum. Because they missed their entry point, each big leg higher only pushed them deeper into the psychological funk that strengthens their resolve to continue to wait for the re-test.

What they're waiting for wouldn't be a dip. It would have to be something the market has never seen before. Since the Dow bottomed at 6,600 and rallied to 27,000, it would take a crash of 20,400 points or a 76% pullback!

The dip you seek is often an excuse for not getting a price you had the chance for but didn't take. I always say *it's not about chasing stocks but chasing fundamentals.* Forget about this rearview mirror stuff and your fragile ego. Let's focus on the future and positioning you for Unstoppable Prosperity. Besides, when you reach that end, I promise your ego will be just fine.

Since we know that dips will happen, you need to be prepared to move. When the dip comes, make sure you buy great stocks with depressed prices because of the overall downturn in the market. They need to be stocks that you've researched and in which you have confidence.

I'm not saying you should be able to pick the bottom. But I don't want you to be that person who needs to see the market reverse to new highs before "knowing" the worst is over.

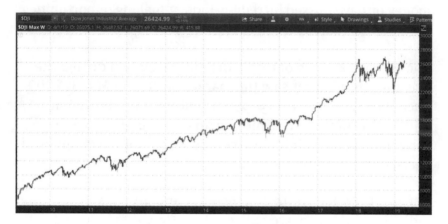

Gaming your investments around only stock market dips is folly and a huge risk to your long-term goal of creating wealth. If you had waited to enter this last bull market, you can see there were very few dips to take advantage of and you would've missed out on most of a great run.

First, it's hard to buy dips anyway. When you're in a plane and it hits an air pocket, dreadful thoughts cross your mind. While investing isn't life or death, when the stock market turns lower and there's a huge down session, very few investors are looking to buy. For most, it's a victory just to hold onto stocks in great companies when everyone else seems to be selling.

Buying dips can supercharge your returns. It's not something we wait for but, when it happens, we try to take advantage because it supercharges your long-term returns.

MISTAKE #6 - BUYING ONLY ONE STOCK

I've lost track of how many times someone has told me he or she was in the market and it didn't work out, with the implication being that they're done with it.

The irony is they approached the stock market in a way that resulted in their worst fears and negative assumptions about the stock market being realized due to their approach!

Invariably, I ask about their experience. In most cases it turns out they took a shot on a tip or their own hunch and bought shares in a single stock.

Interestingly, most of their stories have the share price initially going higher but then eventually turning lower. That's when the would-be investor decided to pull the plug and close the position at a loss, vowing never to try it again.

These folks never had a plan when they bought the stock, other than assuming it would move higher and higher into infinity. Mostly, however, they set themselves up to prove the elites were right all the time; the stock market wasn't for them. It was over their heads and too complicated, or too rigged, or too much work. But they never blame themselves for a lack of planning and discipline.

This is like most visitors to Las Vegas or Atlantic City. Many years ago, I went to the latter with a friend who wanted to stay longer than originally planned and since he drove, I decided to take a bus home.

It was such a downer. Not the ride home but the bus station itself. It was filled with all these long faces of gamblers with barely enough money left to get back home.

I began asking a few people what happened. What I found was very informative. Every single person was up at one point but couldn't decide when to stop. Every single person in that bus station planned to come back and win everything back.

How interesting that people see more wisdom in rolling the dice with their hard-earned money for random results than investing in the stock market. They can lose over and over and keep coming back. I guess there's something there for them. The shows are great, the food is getting better, and the lights are mesmerizing. What isn't there... is Unstoppable Prosperity.

Those would be, one-shot investors unwilling to learn how to invest and manage risk have the same kind of chances of success as the weekend gamblers in Las Vegas.

MISTAKE #7 - LETTING THE NEWS GET YOU DOWN

There are always challenges in everyday life that create a world of worry. The same is true with our country and the world we inhabit. It feels these days that it's worse than ever, but it really isn't. We just have the means to hear all the challenges and the opinions about those challenges.

We see each storm and every local flood. Events that most Americans might not have heard about in 1970 go viral today. On the political front it seems like things are more hopeless than ever and we're on the cusp of a Constitutional crisis.

Investing against this backdrop may seem hard but it's not impossible. It just means that you must do your own work and know the facts and fundamental underpinnings of the economy as well as your individual positions.

NOW YOU KNOW

So many mistakes aren't about a lack of knowledge but rather falling victim to our emotions. We make our worst fears come true in life, and in the stock market, by the actions we take or don't take. It's self-fulfilling. So many of the mistakes are simply sulking and self-pity, crawling into a fetal position rather than keeping your head high, not only to weather financial storms but to benefit from them as well.

Reacting to mistakes can compound the outcome making it worse. In fact, it's okay to make mistakes. They aren't deliberate. But when your reaction compounds and makes the outcome worse than it has to be **then** you're making bad decisions.

Mistakes are forgivable. Bad decisions are less forgivable and more costly for investors.

The easiest example is when greed stops an investor from taking profits and soon a big winner has turned lower and the stock is simply at breakeven. Perhaps underlying fundamentals have changed but many investors feel that a higher price was ordained, or they feel dumb for missing it.

It's a bad decision now to hold a stock where the value proposition has changed but investors sulk and wed themselves to the position even as it becomes a loser.

Knowledge is the key around these emotional mistakes. Losses will happen and setbacks are an inevitable part of life and investing. As you focus on your goal of Unstoppable Prosperity dealing with setbacks and losses becomes a lot easier.

NOW EXECUTE

Avoiding mistakes can often be achieved by two things:

- Using your knowledge
- Controlling your emotions

To do that successfully and consistently you need to be self-aware. You must be honest with yourself and avoid letting your ego color the reality of any situation. These are not easy things to do. We need to occasionally step back and look honestly at decisions we've made and evaluate how we did.

Look back on a stock that didn't perform as well as you'd hoped. Look back at the fundamentals and pull up some old charts. Determine what happened. Did you make a mistake by getting caught up in the hype or hanging on to a loser too long? Did you miss something in the fundamentals or in the general economy? Mistakes are not embarrassments but rather learning experiences, if we use them properly.

Write down what you learn from this exercise. Writing it down will help clarify your thinking, help you learn for the next time and avoid costly mistakes.

EIGHT

CHAPTER

FUNDAMENTALS: A DEEPER DIVE

At this point you should have enough information to start to take charge of your own investments and begin your road to Unstoppable Prosperity. Whether you're an experienced trader or investor or you're newer to the market, I highly recommend you dig deeper into the stocks that are on your Watch List after they pass your quick fundamental and technical analysis.

Investors looking for greater confirmation about their holdings or potential investments should dig even deeper to assess and formulate the value proposition. This is especially true of long-time investors in the stock market that've never had a formal methodology when it comes to buying and selling.

Many go by the "story" often voiced through the media or a friend. This approach has resulted in very uneven results and lots of frustration.

Knowledge is power. So, while I know I've supplied tools to help make you successful, for those that want to go even deeper for greater knowledge this is where we begin the deeper dive.

All publicly traded companies are required to provide financial reporting to both their shareholders and the Securities and Exchange Commission (SEC). They have this information posted on their corporate site or you can search for it on the SEC's website here: https://www.sec.gov/edgar/searchedgar/companysearch.html.

DEEPER FUNDAMENTAL ANALYSIS: COMPANY TRENDS

Imagine if you saved up money for ten years with the goal of one day owning a restaurant and there were three in your town up for sale.

- They all were about the same size
- They all had similar menus
- They all seemed to be successful

You'd need to do your research. The first thing you'd ask all the owners is to look at their books. Those "books" are financial documents that provide insight into just how successful the company has been in the past and helps you formulate how much growth there could be in the future.

You'd assess risks and spot any red flags immediately (like maybe why the owner's nephew is making $100,000 with no job description) to guard against your own eagerness to be a restaurant owner. You're excited to get started. You have ideas and understand that we live in a world of food voyeurism and changing taste that people are willing to pay a premium for. All of that may be true but we can't lose sight of the practical issues.

The business will still have to execute and must operate in a manner that generates profits. It's a lot easier looking from the outside to assume success. But it's a never-ending challenge. Getting to the top and staying at the top means commitment, innovation and execution.

That's not the glamorous side of the business and the would-be restaurant buyer must take care to understand that while they may love the ambiance of the restaurant, it must make money.

Of course, publicly traded companies are a lot more complicated businesses than local restaurants, but the premise is the same. And just as with the fictional restaurant, you want to look at the books.

With fundamental analysis we're about to make critical assessments:

- Is the business growing?
- Are profits improving?
- Is management positioning the company for future success?
- Is the company beating or gaining on competitors?
- Is the company generating cash to fund growth and reward investors?
- Is the company managing debt?

Every industry has its own measures, or metrics, that give us ways to determine the winners and potential winners. Meanwhile, there are several ways to measure all industries and individual companies to determine the best investment proposition. First, we measure the company against itself to understand what it has achieved and what it can achieve. We can then measure current circumstances against those parameters.

In Chapter 2, I explained how current events and curiosity should spark you to consider economic implications and eventually how you can make money. We find intriguing companies and put them on a Watch List and then look for certain developments. We can measure these developments with quick fundamental and technical analysis that work.

Those quick analytic techniques can help you decide on a stock that just hit your radar and perhaps is on the verge of a major rally. But when making normal investing decisions, you want to drill deeper and know more because it's your hard-earned money and future prosperity. This deeper knowledge will make you a much better investor and allow you to avoid so many emotional pitfalls that destroy investors (professional and novice). It's also a key tool that helps you find the winners.

I'm going to use examples of different stocks throughout this chapter as I teach you the process of the fundamental deep dive.

BUYING AND SELLING BASED ON FORWARD PE VALUATION

Wall Street analysts and TV pundits focus on the Price to Earnings (PE) ratio as the preferred gauge to determine valuation. I consider it a major mistake as it focuses on the prior twelve months of earnings. Investors, on the other hand, are forward-looking and thus the prior twelve months are not nearly as important to them as the next twelve months and beyond. We discussed the importance of future earnings trends during our quick fundamental analysis in Chapter 2.

For this reason, I prefer to look at the share price versus the next twelve months of earnings by using the forward PE ratio rather than dwell on valuations based on the past twelve months.

Here's the difference:

Price to Earnings

- Formula = current share price / earnings per share for the previous 12 months

Forward Price to Earnings or Forward PE Ratio

- Formula = current share price / consensus future earnings per share

Earnings per Share

- Formula = net income – preferred dividends / weighted average shares outstanding

Note: There are numerous websites and apps that offer free access to forward PE ratios, trailing twelve-month PE ratios and earnings per share (eps).

Buybacks as a Wild Card

Since we are looking ahead and trying to gauge real value, we have to look at earnings but also consider how many shares are outstanding in the public float.

The "float" is a term that describes the total number of shares that are available to be traded. It's different than "shares outstanding" which is the total number of shares held by all investors. Float is found by subtracting "restricted shares" from the number of shares outstanding. Restricted shares are those that while part of the total shares outstanding, are not available to be traded at this time for various reasons.

I know old school market purists hate stock buybacks and for some companies it has been a poor use of cash, from IBM to GameStop, shareholders would have been better served with business investments or relevant acquisitions. To be clear, a stock buyback is simply the repurchasing of shares from shareholders by the company at current market value.

Some fret that this is financial engineering or essentially gimmickry, but others say it's just one of two ways the company rewards shareholders. The other is increasing the quarterly dividend. Most companies do both and we may see greater dividend increases and slower stock buybacks in a political climate looking to raise government revenues.

Either way, these buybacks have most certainly made a difference in share prices and will continue to, so it's another item on the checklist of self-directed investors that should be checked out. While buyback announcements aren't binding, most companies not only live up to them but eventually increase them. This is true even in bad times for the company and the economy.

The fact of the matter is that a major driver of the market has been buybacks and takeovers which means fewer companies and higher value per shares outstanding. For the most part, I hope and think these buybacks will continue for years to come.

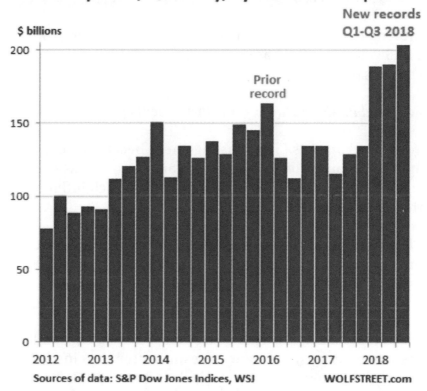

Share Buybacks, Quarterly, by S&P 500 Companies

Source: https://wolfstreet.com/2018/12/18/stocks-suffer-nasty-quarter-after-record-share-buybacks/

The most important thing to remember about the stock market is that for all the noise and occasionally hot new investing or trading approach, including the use of machines, share price is ultimately determined by earnings growth.

This is critical to remember in this era of the market where more companies are using their own funds to buy back their own shares which makes the overall share float even smaller.

Fewer shares in the float (pool of shares available to public) magnifies earnings.

Example:

$10 in total earnings into 10 shares = $1.00 eps

$10 in total earnings into 8 shares = $1.25 eps

Although the total dollar amount is the same, earnings of $1.25 will move the share price of the stock higher than earnings of $1.00.

Forward PE Case Study: *Texas Instruments (TXN)*

Texas Instruments (TXN) management became a very aggressive buyer of its own shares and that produced a significant impact on earnings per share which influenced the stock price significantly higher.

There were great periods of growth and execution, but the one constant was aggressive share buybacks which made the float smaller and smaller and magnified earnings which helped to nudge the stock higher.

On October 21, 2015 TXN shares closed at $51.90 and the company posted financial results after the close of trading. The next day the stock closed at $58.98. So, was the stock worth 14% more after that earnings result and guidance? For me the answer is no. I would not have chased the stock.

Using the future to determine value and when to buy, sell or hold:

1. Revenues don't matter. TXN revenue growth, or lack thereof, didn't stop the shares from rallying from $51.90 on October 21, 2015 to $71.42 on July 26, 2016.

2. Margin expansion gives management the luxury of applying cash to investments or buybacks.

3. Free cash flow is critical as this is the normal source of funds used in returning cash to shareholders. Free cash flow is derived from cash from operations minuses capital expenditures.

4. PE ratios don't matter.

5. Forward PE ratios, however, are big factors to determine whether to buy, hold, or sell. Here are hard rules that will curb your greed and offset your urge to take excessive risk:

   Rules for Technology Stocks:
   • Forward PE Under 15 = Buy Signal
   • Forward PE Over 20 = Sell Signal

6. Management Guidance keeps investors ahead of the Wall Street consensus. I always use the upper end of the range provided by management and compare it to the same quarter results from one year earlier. These are soft rules but great guidelines:

   • Negative earnings guidance = sell
   • Unchanged up to 15% guidance = hold
   • Over 15% guidance = buy

TXN Financial Results

Report Date	Oct 21, 2015	Jan 27, 2016	Apr 27, 2016	Jul 25, 2016	Oct 26, 2016	Jan 24, 2017	Apr 25, 2017	Jul 25, 2017	Oct 24, 2017	Jan 23, 2018	Apr 24, 2018	Jul 24, 2018
Quarter Results	3Q 2015	4Q 2015	1Q 2016	2Q 2016	3Q 2016	4Q 2016	1Q 2017	2Q 2017	3Q 2017	4Q 2017	1Q 2018	2Q 2018
Price Before	$51.90	$50.67	$59.92	$66.22	$71.71	$77.08	$82.36	$81.39	$96.44	$119.89	$98.42	$113.80
Closing Price Next Day	$58.09	$51.13	$58.69	$71.42	$70.73	$78.58	$81.11	$82.53	$95.82	$109.70	$103.00	$113.22
Revenue	-2%	-2%	-5%	+1%	+7%	+7%	+13%	+13%	+12%	+10%	+11%	+9%
Gross Margin	58.2	58.5	60.6	61.2	62.0	62.5	63.0	64.3	64.5	65.1	64.6	65.2
Free Cash Flow	+4% $3.6b	+6% $3.7b	+11% $3.7b	+17% $3.9b	+8% $3.9b	+6% $4.1b	+11% $4.2b	Unchanged $4.0b	+4% $4.2b	+14% $4.7b	+17% $4.9b	+42% $5.7b
Earnings Per Share	$0.76 Unchanged	$0.80 +5%	$0.65 +7%	$0.76 +17%	$0.94 +24%	$1.02 +28%	$0.97 +41%	$1.03 +30%	$1.26 +29%	$0.34 -67%	$1.35 +39%	$1.40 +36%
PE (trailing)	19.2/21.4	18.7/18.7	21.6/21.2	23.0/24.8	23.4/23.1	23.9/24.3	19.2/21.4	18.7/18.7	21.6/21.2	23.0/24.8	23.4/23.1	23.9/24.3
PE (forward)	9.25/10.51	9.03/9.11	10.6/10.4	11.8/12.7	12.7/12.6	13.7/14.0	14.4/14.6	14.5/14.7	17.1/17.0	22.8/20.9	18.7/19.6	21.6/21.5
Guidance vs 1 Year Ago	0.74 -2.6%	$0.80 +9.8%	$0.65 +18.5%	$0.76 +19.7%	$0.94 +7.5%	$1.02 +27.5%	$1.01 +32.9%	$1.18 +20.4%	$1.15 +12.7%	$1.17 +20.6%	$1.39 25.9%	$1.63 +29.4%

Reading Financial Releases

Forget self-serving superlatives and focus on numbers. Look for companies that talk about market share gains and major shakeups in their businesses.

Guidance is critical. Most companies offer a range and I always take the high end of that range for modelling. In this case, management offered current quarterly earnings in a range of $0.89 to $1.01. We take that higher number $1.01 and compare to actual results in the quarter a year earlier.

For example, in the second quarter of 2016 TXN earned $0.76, so management was signaling a 32.9% increase for the current quarter 2Q 2017.

Texas Instruments reported 1Q17 financial results and shareholder returns:

> DALLAS, April 25, 2017 /PRNewswire/ -- Texas Instruments Incorporated (TI) (NASDAQ: TXN) today reported first-quarter revenue of $3.40 billion, net income of $997 million and earnings per share of 97 cents. Earnings per share include an 8-cent discrete tax benefit not in the company's original guidance.

> Regarding the company's performance and returns to shareholders, Rich Templeton, TI's chairman, president and CEO, made the following comments:

> "Revenue increased 13 percent from the same quarter a year ago. Demand for our products continued to be strong in the automotive market and continued to strengthen in the industrial market.

> "In our core businesses, Analog revenue grew 20 percent and Embedded Processing revenue grew 10 percent from

the same quarter a year ago. Operating margin increased in both businesses.

"Gross margin of 63.0 percent reflected the quality of our product portfolio, as well as the efficiency of our manufacturing strategy, including the benefit of 300-millimeter Analog production.

"Our cash flow from operations of $4.8 billion for the trailing 12 months again underscored the strength of our business model. Free cash flow for the trailing 12 months was up 11 percent from a year ago to $4.2 billion and represents 30.7 percent of revenue, up from 29.5 percent a year ago.

"We have returned $3.8 billion to owners in the past 12 months through stock repurchases and dividends.

"Our balance sheet remains strong with $3.0 billion of cash and short-term investments at the end of the quarter, about 80 percent of which was owned by the company's U.S. entities. Inventory ended the quarter at 132 days.

"TI's second-quarter outlook is for revenue in the range of $3.40 billion to $3.70 billion, and earnings per share between $0.89 and $1.01, which includes an estimated $30 million discrete tax benefit."

TXN Assessment

When TXN posted results on October 21, 2015 I wouldn't have bought the stock based on guidance that was going to see earnings as a best-case scenario according to management that were lower than the prior year comparison. The January 27, 2016 release saw gross margin climb to a company record and free cash flow increase nicely, but forward guidance of $0.80 was only 9.8% better.

This was a sign for current shareholders to hold but not enough to trigger a fresh buy signal. The April 27, 2016 report was the ultimate buy signal. Shares were changing hands at the same valuation as the day after the October 21, 2015 release but guidance was a robust 18.5% higher than year earlier earnings per share and free cash flow (which could be used to buy back more shares) increased at an even faster rate.

Your entry point: $58.69

Additional Buy Points

- July 25, 2016 report (see earnings guidance) @ $71.42
- January 24, 2017 report (see earnings guidance and low forward PE) @ $78.58

Let's pause here and reflect. Using this approach to valuation and future potential valuations based on management's guidance, investors could have bought the stock at $58.69 and more than a year later at $78.58. In fact, there was greater conviction to own the stock after that January 24, 2017 report than the five quarters prior.

The stock flashed fresh buy signals ($82.92 and $82.53) until the Oct 24, 2017 results where guidance only climbed 12.7%, enough to hold but not enough to create a new position.

Sell Signal

Soon shareholders would get the first sell signal based on forward PE ratio. On January 5, 2018 shares of TXN were changing hands at $109.12 or forward PE of 20.06. That is a sell signal particularly for investors with emotional issues tied to closing positions at gains or losses.

Remember #5 on our guidelines for exiting based on rising forward PE ratios?

5. Forward PE ratios, however, are big factors to determine whether to buy, hold, or sell. Here are hard rules that will curb your greed and offset your urge to take excessive risk:

Rules for Technology Stocks:
- Forward PE Under 15 = Buy Signal
- Forward PE Over 20 = Sell Signal

Closing the position here would have made every buy signal (5 signals in total) entry point based on guidance and forward PE valuation profitable:

86%

54%

39%

32%

32%

Below is a chart of TXN showing the stock performance since 2015:

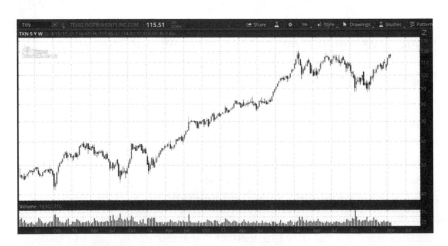

Buy Signal

Although forward guidance was huge, including 25.9% in April and 29.4% in July 2018, the forward PE ratio was too high so investors focused on valuations would have had to wait things out.

The next buy signal came with financial earnings results posted on October 23, 2018. The stock reacted by selling off by more than $10.00 by the end of the week. This knocked the forward PE ratio down to 17.50. With the forward PE back under 20 and the guidance over 15%, this fell back into my buy zone.

TXN Financial Results	
Report Date	Oct 23, 2018
Quarter Results	3Q 2018
Price Before	$100.25
Closing Price Next Day	$92.01
Revenue	+4%
Gross Margin	65.8
Free Cash Flow	+4.0% $5.9B
Earnings Per Share	$1.34
PE (trailing)	19.66
PE (forward)	19.50 / 17.5
Guidance vs 1 Year Ago	$1.34 +16.5%

INCOME STATEMENT

Let's move on to the income statement. How much money is coming in through sales and how much of it reaches the bottom line?

On November 4, 2016, MasTec (MTZ) posted its financial results for its third quarter, which ended on the last business day in September.

It was a monster quarter, signaling a big turnaround and shift in momentum. Sales were strong, margins soared, and billings pointed to continued strong revenue growth in the future.

MasTec (MTZ) 3Q Financial Results	2016	2015	Checking the company against the same period in the prior year is the initial step in fundamental analysis.
Revenue	$1,586,181	$1,111,010	Revenue +42.8% (the year before it was -15.5% in the same quarter.)
Gross Margin	13.7%	12.4%	Gross margins include costs that are often out of management's control, so improvement here is impressive.
Operating Margin	6.0%	1.2%	**This is my favorite metric of all. My number one investment axiom: when margins expand, price of stock moves higher.**
Billings	$559.3	$437.3	A glimpse of future, potential revenue.
Cash Flow from Op	$78,086,000	($2,766,000)	Cash flow is king and assessing future flows is how many money managers select their investments.
Earnings per Share	$0.69	$0.09	This is the number that gets all attention and moves the stock market.

There's no doubt the year to year performance in the third quarter screamed "buy this stock." If a potential investor wanted to really understand how great the quarter was and why it signaled the coast is clear, he could stretch the evaluation period over several years.

Remember the key disclaimer in investing: "Past performance is not a guarantee of future results."

That disclaimer is designed to provide legal coverage for the industry, but it also underscores the reality that there can be fluke periods. This year's hot money manager could go on to be next year's worst. Maybe you had a hunch that worked once and made you a bunch of money that has since failed. These things happen in both a negative and positive manner. Sometimes a company gets "lucky" and has a good quarter through no "fault" of their own. Part of what I'm doing in this book is teaching you to limit the impact of these flukes. The thing that mitigates the impact of a fluke is to know longer-term trends.

This is especially true in business where performance is informed by demand for products, industry trends and management's ability to execute (beat its rivals and steer the company toward ever-improving performance).

With this in mind, I went back over recent years to see if the MTZ great 2016 third quarter was a positive fluke or part of a greater long-term trend that wasn't accidental or temporary.

Revenue Changes

Revenue growth erupted in the third quarter 2016, surging at a faster pace than any time in the previous five years. I also saw that the company had reversed a big slide that had occurred before the five-year period I was looking at in detail. The ability for management to reverse a multi-year slide would contribute, big time, to our "buy signal."

2016: +42.8%
2015: -15.5%
2014: +3.2%
2013: +18.9%
2012: +30.8%

Once we've seen that the revenue was up year over year, we need to drill down deeper to see where the growth is coming from.

All large companies have more than one business segment to drive overall revenue and profits.

Ideally, the largest business segment will also be enjoying the largest profit margins. In some cases that might not be true, in part because of the maturity of the product or service. In those cases, we want to see that the fastest growing part of the business will also enjoy the best profit margins and those margins are still growing.

When revenues and profits margins are increasing, it results in greater earnings before interest and taxes. It's common to include depreciation and amortization when analyzing cash flow for a more accurate number. Earnings before interest, taxes, depreciation and amortization (EBITDA) is Wall Street's preferred way to measure cash flow.

Measuring segment operating margins and EBITDA (Cash Flow)

To get a better idea on business trends and opportunities, investors must go "micro," which is a fancy word for a smaller, more focused look at the business and its individual segments.

This micro look means we drill down deeper to see where the growth and profits are coming from. We need to analyze the revenue trends.

In this case, each of the MTZ business segments enjoyed strong year over year revenue growth. We analyzed revenue growth, margin changes and cash flow (EBITDA). For MasTec (MTZ) the improvement was eye-popping in a couple of segments. Those segments reached record levels.

A comparison of third quarter performance over a five-year period saw several highlights:

- Communication regained upside momentum after declining in 2014.

- Oil and Gas surged 159% over five years to establish a record and become the top business segment.

- The Power segment business revenue was still down from 2012 but trending in a positive direction.

MasTec (MTZ) 3Q Financial Results Business Segments	2016	2015	2014	2013	2012
Communications	$624.3	$513.3	$505.2	$543.0	$490.0
Oil & Gas	$736.0	$406.9	$554.4	$519.1	$284.0
Electrical	$101.7	$75.9	$138.4	$118.8	$74.8
Power	$123.6	$115.0	$114.3	$85.1	$211.7

Millions of USD

MasTec (MTZ) 3Q Financial Results Segment EBITDA (Cash Flow)	2016	2015	2014	2013	2012
Communications	$62.8	$49.7	$52.5	$71.8	$59.5
Oil & Gas	$117.8	$51.0	$73.4	$68.1	$29.0
Electrical	($8.3)	($23.7)	$18.5	$12.1	$10.5
Power	$6.1	$4.8	$4.9	$(6.4)	$4.9

Millions of USD

MasTec (MTZ) 3Q Financial Results EBITDA Margin	2016	2015	2014	2013	2012
Communications [2]	10.1%	9.7%	10.4%	13.2%	12.1%
Oil & Gas [1]	16.0%	12.5%	13.2%	13.1%	10.2%
Electrical [4]	-3.7%	-15.2%	13.4%	10.2%	14.1%
Power [3]	4.9%	4.2%	4.3%	-7.5%	-14.6%

The first thing that pops out is that EBITDA margins (percentage of revenue that becomes cash flow) improved in each business segment – that's huge and speaks to management's ability to address multiple business issues.

When I'm doing this level of analysis (which is always preferable to just relying on a Quick Look), I have certain things I look for and certain steps I take.

1. I look at the biggest sector to see its profitability. In this case it was Oil and Gas. Revenue increased 81% year over year to $736.0 million and EBITDA of $117.8 million was a record 16% of revenue. In the prior year, Oil and Gas revenue declined 26.6% and EBITDA was just 12.5% of revenue.

2. Communications was the second largest revenue segment. It was up 21.6% to $624.3 million and EBITDA (cash flow) reversed a multi-year trend of lower results and shrinking margins. The EBITDA margin bounced to 10.1% in 3Q 2016 after dwindled to just 9.7% in the comparable period of the prior year.

   EBITDA margins came in at 13.2% in third quarter 2014, which means there could be more upside improvement if management continued to execute.

3. The company's Electrical segment lost money but less than the prior year.

   While we want to see all business segments make money, this turn could have been the start of a longer-term trend. Meanwhile, investors would note it's the smallest of the four business segments.

4. Power enjoyed its third consecutive year of revenue improvement for the quarter although $123.6 million was -41.6% less than 3Q 2012. But, remember the old line, "*It's not what you make, it's what you keep.*"

EBITDA, or cash flow, for 3Q 2016 was better than any time in the prior four years. Management found a way to focus on profitable business opportunities in the Power segment. This leads to fatter margins, which leads to higher share price.

The company's largest and fastest growing business segment also enjoyed the fastest and largest cash flow growth. Can you say, "Screaming Buy?"

Other business segments saw improvements in revenue and/or cash flow that added to the impression that management had turned the company around. There was enough business momentum to augment the case for investing in the company stock.

So far with MTZ, we've looked at execution improvement coupled with increases in Wall Street earnings estimates to come up with an initial analysis and reason to buy the stock. But we didn't stop there.

We went deeper to see where the growth and cash flow were coming from and found multiple buy signals. All of this convinced me this stock would be a "buy." But we can also drill deeper. This additional work would be to determine whether to buy (or sell or hold, for that matter) this particular company. The additional work would aid us in assessing risk.

Remember, long-term investing is about knowing the risk. There's macro risk which includes the economy (which is out of the control of management) and competition. There's also the risk about the quality of revenue. For that last one I prefer when companies aren't overly reliant on a few customers because losing one could be devastating.

CUSTOMER BASE RISK

We watch things like consumer confidence and sentiment numbers along with government data on jobs and wages to keep the pulse of potential customers. For some companies, the customer base is narrow and that brings its own set of risks. If one customer runs into problems, it could be a big hit. For instance, MTZ has relied on a handful of customers for up to 75% of its revenue.

Of course, landing these customers can cause a seismic shift in business fortunes just as losing them would also dramatically alter the investment thesis.

MTZ saw a major spike in its Oil and Gas revenue from a contract with Energy Transfer (a consortium of energy companies led by Sunoco) but lost a large contract with Enbridge. While these developments weren't enough to change my opinion that the stock was a buy, it would add more urgency to close the position when other signs suggested positive business trends were slowing or had peaked.

MTZ Large Clients	2016	2015	2014	2013	2012	2012
AT&T	30%	31%	16%	16%	17%	23%
DirecTV			12%	13%	16%	22%
Enbridge	0	0	10%	20%	10%	20%
Energy Transfer	35%	7%	0	0	0	0

BALANCE SHEET

There's so much about the health of the business that you can see on the balance sheet. The three things individual investors should watch are:

- Working Capital
- Manageable debt levels
- Steady inventory (a spike in inventory is a major red flag)

The business needs positive cash flow to operate. This means accounts receivable should be larger than accounts payable to avoid negative cash flow. In addition to wanting accounts receivable (AR) to be larger than accounts payable (AP), the former should be collected faster than the latter is paid out.

Potential Flow of Cash	Designation of Funds	Position on Balance Sheet
Accounts Receivable	To be Collected	Asset
Accounts Payable	To be Paid	Liability

This equation of AR and AP play a major role in formulating Working Capital.

Working Capital = difference between total current assets and total current liabilities. In the case of MTZ in the third quarter 2016, these numbers were very healthy.

Accounts Receivable: $1,215,954,000 up from $911,106 at start of year ($559.3 million billings, +27.9%)

Total Current Assets: $1,422,427,000 up from $1,129,758,000

Accounts Payable: $435,652,000 up from $348,543,000 at start of the year

Total Current Liabilities: $942,365,000 up from $752,575,000

The company posted earnings results that blew away Wall Street consensus and, in the process, showed strong cash flow and improved margins. Every aspect of the earnings trends and reports were superb.

Management raised its guidance for the full year above Wall Street consensus.

- $5.1 billion
- EPS $1.73
- EBITDA $455 million

This stock was a screaming buy at this point but investors looking for greater comfort would make the next step. After all, without some more research we might just be looking at a hot sector. There might be better investments out there in the same sector.

DEEPER FUNDAMENTAL ANALYSIS: PEER REVIEW

I knew this would be a hot sector and put several names on my Watch List. While MTZ stood out the most, I wanted to look throughout the industry to see if any of the peer companies presented an even better investment proposition.

Note: Because these are large corporations, progress is measured in tiny fractions on Wall Street known as 'Basis Points.' A basis point equals 1/100th of 1.0%. It can also be presented as 0.01% or 0.0001.

So, it would take 100 basis points, or bps, to equal one percent.

It's not unlike the Olympics where the fastest man in the world is less than the blink of an eye faster than the guy that comes in fourth place and doesn't win a medal. Check out fastest times in history. Only one of these guys is considered the fastest man in the world:

- Usain Bolt 9.58 seconds
- Tyson Gay 9.69 seconds
- Asafa Powell 9.72 seconds

Likewise, companies can be separated by the smallest of margins. But those margins can make a huge difference in your portfolio. One way to "race" these companies against one another is through a peer review. That's exactly what I decided to do with MasTec (MTZ). I found several companies in the same sector and compared them to MTZ. The first was Emcor.

Peer #1: EMCOR (EME)

EMCOR posted record revenue and strong backlog although the rate of growth wasn't as robust as MasTec. In each line of the income statement, MTZ enjoyed better and stronger results.

EMCOR (EME) 3Q Financial Results	2016	Change	MTZ
Revenue	$1.92b	+12.9%	+42.8%
Gross Margin	13.9%	Unchanged	13.7%
Operating Margin	2.7%	+20 bps	6.0%
Billings	$467.1m	+8.8%	+27.9%
Cash from Operations	$128.9m	+34.8%	+$75m
Diluted Earnings per Share	$0.85	+$0.19	+$0.60

EME's revenue was +12.9% versus MTZ's at +42.8%.

The gross margin was lower for MTZ, but they showed an improvement of +130 basis points year over year.

MTZ's operating margin dwarfed EME's after climbing 480 basis points.

MTZ's billings were greater at $559.3 million and grew 400% faster.

MTZ's cash from operations climbed to $72 million after a loss of almost $3.0 million a year earlier.

MTZ's earnings improved by $0.60 from a year earlier. The percentage change was +667% against just 28% improvement for EME.

The bottom line for this "race" was that while EME was attractive, changes at MTZ were more impressive. Because of its solid showing, I would continue to keep EME on my Watch List and consider it as a buy in the future. But there was more that I wanted to look at.

SEGMENT BUSINESS GROWTH

While not always comparable, it's important to assess sources of revenue during peer reviews to find companies with the most growth and market share in the most lucrative business segments.

EME revenue improved in each business segment except Industrial.

EMCOR (EME) 3Q Financial Results Business Segments	2016	2015
Electronics	$458.6	$344.4
Mechanical	$697.7	$587.5
Building	$454.8	$428.3
Industrial	$239.1	$241.9

Millions of USD

Business segment operating margin trends increased in each business segment but Electrical.

EMCOR (EME) 3Q Financial Results Segment Margins	2016	2015
Electrical	6.7%	7.4%
Mechanical	5.7%	4.6%
Building	5.0%	3.7%
Industrial	6.1%	5.4%

I now had additional information I could use with my Watch List for this company. MasTec was still the better buy, but Emcor was certainly worth adding to my Watch List for the future. I went through the same process again with a second peer company, Quanta Services (PWR).

Peer #2: Quanta Services (PWR)

While not completely apples to apples, Quanta's two main businesses overlap MTZ business segments. The first red flag I saw was the decline in earnings. PWR is a larger company but it's clear MTZ enjoyed much faster growth.

Quanta Services (PWR) 3Q Financial Results	2016	2015
Revenue	$2.04b	$1.94b
Gross Margin	14.8	12.1
Operating Margin	6.3%	4.1%
Backlog: Electrical	$3.36b	$3.31b
Backlog: Oil & Gas	$2.40b	$1.90b
Diluted Earnings per Share	$1.17	$1.22

Quanta Services (PWR) 3Q Financial Results Business Segments	2016	2015
Electrical	$1.22b	$1.18b
Oil & Gas	$819.6m	$756.3m

Quanta Services (PWR) 3Q Financial Results Segment Margins	2016	2015
Electrical	9.7%	6.5%
Oil & Gas	8.0%	7.8%

Margins improved in both segments, although marginally in the Oil and Gas business. Again, these are encouraging trends but not nearly as impressive as the pace of improvement for MTZ during the same quarterly period. While not a bad "runner," Quanta was not the "sprinter" MasTec was. Finally, I looked at Jacobs Engineering (JEC).

Peer 3: Jacobs Engineering (JEC)

Jacobs Engineering posted the worst results in the industry. Revenue declined 18.0% with three of four business segments lower year to year.

Jacobs Engineering (JEC) 3Q Financial Results	2016	2015
Revenue	$2.64b	$3.12b
Gross Margin	16.3	15.2
Operating Margin	3.1	1.7
Backlog	$18.8b	$18.8b
Cash Flow from Operations	$234m	NA
Diluted Earnings per Share	$0.24	$0.24

Only the Industrial segment saw year to year improvement in top line growth. Meanwhile, during the same quarter that saw a monumental surge in Oil and Gas business for MTZ, there was a sharp decline for JEC.

Jacobs Engineering (JEC) 3Q Financial Results Business Segments	2016	2015
Aerospace	$650.0m	$790.3m
Building	$557.5m	$637.8m
Industrial	$749.1m	$665.9m
Oil	$684.0m	$1.02b

Jacobs Engineering (JEC) 3Q Financial Results Segment Margins	2016	2015
Aerospace	7.2%	7.1%
Building	7.5%	3.7%
Industrial	1.7%	4.2%
Oil	5.0%	3.2%

Margins did improve in three of the four segments. Maybe this would've been enough for shareholders at the time to hold. But for investors with no exposure to the industry, the clear choice was MTZ.

PEER TO PEER TABLES

I want to share absolute numbers to demonstrate that they can be deceiving. It really doesn't mean a lot when a company reports sales of a gazillion dollars if it was better a year ago. What if its closest rival had revenue of two gazillion dollars? That changes things from the point of view of an investor.

We also want to consider the quality of financials. Does the management have the ability to post sales that show pricing power and increasing volume? As you make this deep dive into the fundamentals of a company, this is another area that you can consider. But let's go back for a minute to the MTZ example. I'll sometimes use Peer to Peer Tables to put everything in front of me at once.

Decision-Making Process: Picking the Best of the Bunch

A quick glance of 3Q 2016 results shows PWR with higher margins than MTZ. But remember that when we invest, we're anticipating future trends and results. With that in mind, we need to look at the pace and direction of key metrics such as revenue and operating margin and earnings per share. You could look at gross margins which are important but don't give us an insight into management's ability to control costs and maximize gains.

Execution: Absolute Results	Revenue	Gross margin	Operating Margin	Earnings Share
MTZ	$1.92b	13.7	6.0	$0.78
EME	$1.92b	13.9	2.7	$0.85
PWR	$2.04b	14.8	6.3	$1.17
JEC	$2.64b	16.3	3.1	$0.24

The pace of growth is critical. However, we must take care to make sure there aren't any anomalies or unique, non-recurring factors that might skew the numbers.

It's clear that in the third quarter of 2016, MTZ enjoyed a rate of growth well above its rivals. Revenue grew during the period substantially faster than any of the rivals and operating margins and earnings per share also demonstrated outsized growth.

Execution: Change	Revenue	Gross margin	Operating Margin	Earnings Share
MTZ	+43%	+10.5%	+400%	+667%
EME	+13%	Unchanged	+0.08%	+29%
PWR	+5.3%	+22%	+54%	-0.04%
JEC	-18.0%	+7%	+8%	Unchanged

Another reason for choosing MTZ over PWR and others is the company's strongest growing business, Oil and Gas, improved much better and faster. The other rivals had no exposure to Communication, which has underlying drivers that are sure to generate exponential growth opportunities for the next decade.

NOW YOU KNOW

Publicly traded companies release their financial results to the public every three months. This allows everyone to "look under the hood" and crunch the numbers. When you hear that a company beat Wall Street revenue and earnings consensus, that's great. But how do we really know that revenues up 20% is good, particularly when rivals might be growing revenues 30% and taking market share?

Any company can raise prices. But if higher prices result in fewer sales and less market share, it's a red flag. Consider the example of the U.S. Postal Service. It has the ability to raise the price of postage and has dramatically done so over the years. This has resulted in a smaller and smaller pool of users while driving others to seek alternatives. This is a demonstration of a LACK of pricing power!

When a company sees profits, market share and operating margins improve, the underlying share price is going to move higher. And while you'll hear some experts say financial releases are rearview mirror news, these releases can speak to the future.

In addition to management guidance, financial results underscore and reveal trends that help to establish valuation parameters for the company based on its own historic precedence and valuations within its own peer group.

Taking the extra steps for going deeper on fundamentals will give you more comfort and greater peace of mind as an investor.

That added sense of security means you'll panic less often and even see opportunities when the masses react on emotion. You now have several levels of research approaches and techniques to aid you with your goal of Unstoppable Prosperity.

NOW EXECUTE

I've outlined several additional steps I suggest you take to gain more insight into any potential investment. For this activity, you can choose either a stock you own or one that is on your Watch List. Even better? Do this exercise on several stocks.

Follow the steps I took in my deeper fundamental analysis. Then do a peer review for that stock. The peer review is the step that takes the most time and is often the one investors are reluctant to do. It provides so much additional information that it's well worth the time and effort. Chances are you haven't ever done one before, so now is your chance. I understand it will take a bit of time, but it gets easier and faster the more you do it.

If you've done one before, congratulations, you're ahead of most other investors. But do this exercise anyway. Pick a stock that might be moving laterally rather than up or maybe even in a downward trend. Do a peer review to see if it's performing like the rest of that segment of the market. If not, it may be time to make some tough decisions. At least you'll have good information upon which to base those choices.

CHAPTER NINE

A DEEPER LOOK AT TECHNICALS

In Chapter 3 we began looking at technicals to determine when we want to enter or exit a position. In this chapter, I want to take a look at some other trends that I use to help pinpoint the best times to buy or sell.

Experienced traders know they need a deep understanding of the technicals. When your intent is to make your profit over a short period of time, knowing *when* to buy or sell becomes crucial.

Likewise, experienced investors know that having a deep knowledge of when to buy or sell can increase profits on any position in your portfolio. Investing in companies that are fundamentally sound is still the most crucial decision. But, knowing *when* to move can make the difference in the size of the profit or loss from any transaction.

If you're experienced, or as you gain more experience and become comfortable with reading charts, this chapter provides additional ways to help you make decisions. This is about refining your use of charts to further enhance your technical analysis skills.

Below I've listed some of the additional technical indicators I like to use. You can use as many, or as few, as you feel comfortable with, as long as you don't use them as excuses for not taking action!

- Candlesticks
- Gaps
- Moving Averages (MA)
- Relative Strength Index (RSI)
- Moving Average Convergence/Divergence (MACD)
- Bollinger Bands ®
- Money-Flow Index (MFI)

CANDLESTICKS

Most of the graphs within this book show a chart type known as "candlesticks." They're more straightforward than they first appear. The thin part of the candlestick is referred to as the "wick." The wide portion is known as the "candle body." The wick takes into account the high and low for the day, thus the range of prices the stock traded within during that session. The body focuses on the relationship between the open and close price for the day.

A bullish candle is thought to be one in which the close is greater than the open while it's reversed for a bearish candle. If the close price is less than the open price, that's a bearish candle and the thought process could be something akin to this: "The stock tried to rally that day but ultimately it was driven under its open price so selling likely exceeded buying."

To be clear, the color the body takes on is entirely determined by the relationship of the close to the open and has nothing to do with the closing price of the prior day. The colors of the candles vary based on the platform you're using, and many platforms allow you to customize the color based on your preference. The charts I'm using throughout the book show bullish candles as gray and bearish as black.

Most technicians have adopted the use of candlesticks and there are a lot of unique patterns that can be used for much deeper analysis. However, my main focus is to quickly ascertain if there was more buying than selling or more selling than buying. Candlesticks quickly provide us a visual representation of that.

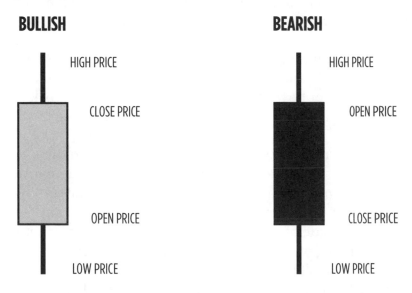

BULLISH

HIGH PRICE

CLOSE PRICE

OPEN PRICE

LOW PRICE

BEARISH

HIGH PRICE

OPEN PRICE

CLOSE PRICE

LOW PRICE

GAPS

Price gaps or "gaps" are areas on a chart where the price action does not overlap from one day to the next. A quick visual will serve us well:

Just like the name indicates, there's a "gap" between the closing price from one day and the opening price for the next.

Typically, a gap is caused by news or rumors that the Street thinks is significant. As we've seen throughout the book, that may or may not be true. However, the action in the stock price is real, even if the information that caused it isn't.

Gaps can occur even when the news is unrelated to the product or service offered by the company. For example, a stock may open lower if there's poor economic news coming out of China even if the company doesn't do any business outside of the USA. This is where having a general understanding of the macro economy helps investors. Things that don't change the fundamental proposition of your stock can have a temporary impact on the share price.

I've seen gaps occur in a stock price because of something that happened to a competitor. And once these gaps occur, the wise investor has to be aware of how behaviorals that we talked about in Chapter 4 can become a force on the stock price. An overreaction to whatever caused the gap can, and often does, occur. It's always a good idea, when you see a gap, to do a quick check to make sure nothing in the fundamentals have changed to cause the gap. If there's been no change and there's no solid reason for the gap, you need to recognize the potential that exists.

Once I know that the fundamental proposition of the company has remained the same, I become excited. I see the opportunity that has just presented itself to me.

Let me create a hypothetical situation to explain how this can be a positive thing for you.

Some news or a rumor hits the market and the overreactions begin. It typically takes the form of selling by those investors who haven't done their homework well enough and just react to the downward trend on the chart. "Momentum traders" (those traders, not investors, who look to make small profits on any movement of a stock price) jump in and put even more pressure on the stock price. With the price down, the financial media "experts" need to provide their audience or readers an explanation. Since bad news is always an easier sell than good news, the *doom sayers* launch into opinions about what this could mean. Of course, these are just opinions. You know better because you've done the work. But this negative influence may result in a downturn in the stock price.

Normally, these situations take a little while to play out because not everyone reacts immediately. However, once that process completes itself and the "last seller has sold," the stock can finally be on the path to recovery. At that point things can get really interesting.

I now have a chance to acquire shares at a reduced price. Since I've already checked to make sure there were no fundamental changes and I know the company is still a sound investment, I act. By doing that, I've improved my position at a discount because I took the time to read the chart.

You may wonder why I would increase my position in a stock that had just shown a gap. I know that gaps are almost always "filled" at a later date. This "filling of a gap" occurs when the price returns to the pre-gap level and even overlaps the "hole."

Again, a visual always works better when it comes to understanding charting:

Notice in the TD chart above how the gap in early December was filled in mid-January. What I know from experience, and now you do too, is that gaps are often filled following this short-lived panic sell-off.

Let me stop right here with a reminder. Before I do anything, I go back and review the fundamentals. It would be nice to know why the gap occurred. If the stock was reacting to news or events that are unrelated to the company, then I have an excellent opportunity. But before I commit to anything, I review the fundamentals. The gap can also be an indicator that something has changed that I might have otherwise missed. If so, I need to reevaluate my position and possibly exit from that position. Gaps are important to note and pay attention to for a number of reasons. But I still get excited when I see them because of the possibilities they usually present.

Let me go back to my example for a minute. Look at the gap labeled "continuation gap" in the chart. This type of gap is identified this way because the gap occurs in the same direction as the trend that was in place at the time. For me, this is important.

I don't focus on gaps being filled while the stock price is moving *away* from the gap. I dial into the gap levels once the stock price has reversed and is heading back in the direction of the gap to close it. In other words, I don't want to fight against the trend when using gaps as target levels. If the price is still falling, I'll be patient and wait until it has turned around and is moving back up towards that point where we can say the gap has been filled. I'm not trying to predict the bottom or hit the exact moment the trend reverses and starts back up. I want to identify *trends*.

At the risk of sounding like I'm nagging, you need to check the fundamentals. Fundamentals of the company need to continue to be strong. If I find information that something significant has changed, I reevaluate. Fundamentals are the key.

MOVING AVERAGES

Another chart trend that I use is "Moving Averages" (MA). Moving averages are one of the most commonly used tools by technical analysts as well as individual and institutional investors.

There are a whole bunch of ways to use them that can provide a lot of valuable information but I'm going to focus on a couple that I really like.

One of the things that moving averages can do is provide support and resistance for prices. Let's do a quick refresher here. Resistance is a price level where a stock seems to stall when it's on an upward trend. Support is a level below which a price seems to not be willing to fall when the price is on a downward trend.

Just like the name implies, moving averages are price averages for a specific number of days in the past. So, the average price for the last 20 days is the 20-Day Moving Average. The price for the last 50 days is the 50-Day Moving average, and so on.

I utilize two that I consider the most critical. They're the 50-Day and 200-Day moving averages. The 20-Day MA is used by some analysts to get a better picture of recent trends. This moving average will be of more value if you're looking at a stock as a trading position and may be moving in and out of the position quickly. From an investor's perspective, the 50-Day and 200-Day moving averages are more useful.

Simple Moving Average (SMA)

Most investors use the Simple Moving Average (SMA). These are basic averages over a specific period of time. There's equal weighting so that each day has the same impact on the average as the next. Most platforms used by investors have moving averages built in so you don't have to do the math. Once you know what the moving average has been for your "look back" period (20 days, 50 days or 200 days), you can compare that to the current stock price.

Here's a view of the 3 Simple Moving Averages on Microsoft (MSFT):

If you're using all three moving averages, and you certainly can, here are some things to consider:

- If the current price falls below the 20-Day average, there isn't a cause for big concerns. The market fluctuates and we know that.

- If you find that the current price falls below the 50-Day average, you should consider that a "yellow flag" and begin to reexamine the fundamentals of the company. This isn't a time to react just yet, but it definitely calls for your attention.

- If you find that the current price falls below the 200-Day average, it calls for immediate action. You must review the company fundamentals and do a historic search to see what news might have occurred that is causing the drop in price. You need to be prepared to act to exit the position if you find that changes have occurred, or the trend doesn't reverse very quickly.

Exponential Moving Average (EMA)

There's another version of the Moving Average, the Exponential Moving Average (EMA). The advantage to using the EMA is that it provides for a weighting of the daily prices. It gives more weight to recent price activity. This might provide just a bit more insight for a stock you aren't quite sure about.

Most platforms offer both moving average types and it's a good idea to have one version or the other, or both, on your charts so that you can see what Wall Street can see. I suggest you work with both before deciding which approach you favor. Just don't forget about the other. Both are very useful "tools" to have in your market tool kit.

I've become comfortable with the Exponential Moving Averages and that's what I use as part of my base charting kit. From time to time though, I'll glance at the simple moving averages to be clear on what price levels the Street is watching.

In a perfect world, chartists prefer to see stock prices on any given day, or number of days, operating above all 3 MAs in bull markets. They do understand that the market fluctuates, and slight misses aren't troublesome. In addition, when everything is going smoothly, we would expect to see the 20-Day MA operating above the 50-Day MA and the 50-Day above the 200-Day. This would be a very strong indication that the stock is heading in a very positive direction.

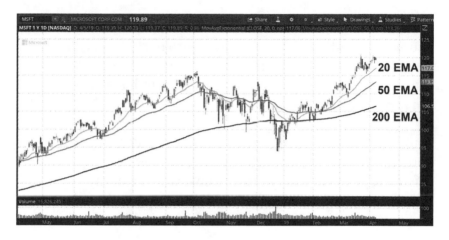

I noted above that if the 200-Day MA fails to hold, when the current price falls below the 200-Day average, there may be issues that we should be concerned about. This is a situation that is very problematic for us.

One of the reasons that we need to watch this closely is that when a stock price falls below the 200-Day average, institutional investors take note and they, collectively, move stock prices around. They're the ones investing hundreds of billions of dollars and those numbers move stock prices. If they're concerned and begin to sell, the price is going to fall. We need to understand why the stock is below the 200-Day MA and be prepared to exit the position if we find a change in the fundamentals or if the price continues to fall.

RELATIVE STRENGTH INDEX (RSI)

RSI is an acronym for the *Relative Strength Index*. This indicator has readings between 0 and 100. Simply put, it measures stock activity over a set period of time. Ideally, we want to see a nice, steady upward trend in the stock price.

If a stock price jumps up too far too fast, the RSI will often produce a reading of over 70. To the experts this is an indication that the stock is being *overbought*. If the RSI reading is under 30, the stock is thought to have fallen too far, too fast and is now *oversold*.

Another way of looking at a stock that is "overbought" is to consider it as being overvalued at the moment and may be due for a pause or a pullback. Conversely, oversold readings can be interpreted as possibly representing undervalued prices that could be due to begin an upward trend.

The RSI line tends to move up and back in cycles swinging between high and low readings in stocks that are producing active movement. Because of that, it's described as an "oscillator" and is also categorized as a "momentum indicator" because it measures the current action of the stock against what it has done in the past.

The RSI is a time-tested, classical technical analysis indicator that can offer lots of signals and insights when used effectively. There are many nuances to the indicator that chartists have catalogued over time but there are two that I always keep my eye out for:

1. Standard overbought/oversold status
2. Divergences – both positive and negative

We'll cover overbought/oversold readings first. Spotting overbought and oversold conditions is fairly straightforward with the RSI. This chart on Microsoft (MSFT) should get the job done for us:

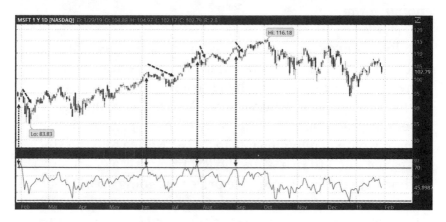

RSI, as well as some other indicators, reside in their own sub-graph below the main price graph.

We need to note a few things about the MSFT chart above. First, notice that in each case where MSFT reached the 70 level (overbought), the stock pulled back. This is exactly why I keep the RSI in my charting mix. It's clear that the stock is overbought at those points and, despite the fact that I may really like MSFT as an investment holding, I know that I'll have a good chance to acquire shares at a lower price level if I'm patient.

If I come upon MSFT looking to buy it, and it's already overbought, I know that it's likely that I'm *late to the party* and should be patient on my entry timing. I've learned to let the stock take a rest. I look to enter once the technical picture has shifted positively and the stock looks primed to start a new push higher.

I want to make one more point with respect to the MSFT chart. Note that the final RSI reading in late August didn't quite make it to the 70 level. I treat these instances as being "close enough for me." I don't get hung-up on it reaching the 70 or 30 level respectively. If the reading gets pretty close and the stock looks like it's about to reverse overall, that's enough for me.

RSI divergences are another way to interpret this indicator and one I've found to be a valuable part of the mix at times. A divergence is registered when the RSI indicator fails to confirm a stock's price movement. Two negative divergences in sequence appeared in Johnson & Johnson prior to the company's stock plunging late in 2018. Notice that the stock price continued to rise while the RSI track was a gradual decline between peaks. So, the price was going up but the demand for the stock was not matching the increase. After the last of these divergences the stock suffered a serious pullback.

When the big institutions are less inclined to want to add shares at higher levels, it may be time to look for better value elsewhere. I return to the fundamentals to see if I still have as much conviction as I once held on a stock that's flashing concerning technical signs such as these.

It's possible to have a positive divergence as well. This would be a "buy indicator" if you were looking to acquire or improve this position.

Cisco Systems (CSCO) provides us with a fine example of positive divergence in the RSI indicator:

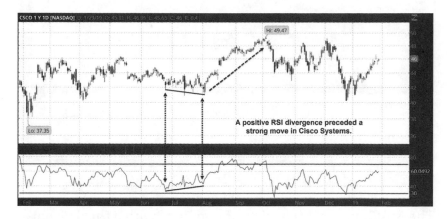

A positive RSI divergence preceded a strong move in Cisco Systems.

MACD – Moving Average Convergence/Divergence Indicator

The MACD indicator is a valuable companion to the RSI indicator. The MACD uses moving averages in clever ways to detect momentum shifts in stock prices. It's often thought to be more effective in trending stocks than the RSI, while the RSI is thought to provide better signals in stocks that are within specific trading ranges. As a result, using both together as a *package deal* is a fairly common approach taken by chartists. I use them in tandem myself.

1 - MACD line **2** - Signal line **3** - Histogram **4** - Zero line

The MACD typically consists of two lines with a third visual feature, known as the "Histogram," included on some platforms. I prefer the version that includes the Histogram.

The first line of the two is the MACD line. It's normally calculated this way:

   12-Day EMA minus 26-Day EMA

The "EMA" in that calculation means that an *exponential moving average* is being used. As I mentioned before, EMAs place greater emphasis on the most recent data used in the calculation. Thus, the past few trading days will weigh more heavily than trading data further in the past. Typically, the closing price for each day is used to calculate the averages used in the MACD on a given stock.

The second line used in the MACD is known as the Signal line. It's calculated as a 9-Day EMA of the MACD line itself. Remember, the MACD line is essentially the difference between the 12 and 26-Day EMAs. So, the Signal line is effectively an average of that average difference.

By design, it lags behind the more responsive MACD line.

Finally, the Histogram is plotted as a visual aid so that the user can more easily recognize the difference/distance between the MACD line and the Signal line as they converge and diverge from one another. This is indicated by bars above and below what is called the Zero line. When the price momentum (as per the MACD's calculations) is becoming negative, the Histogram will show below the Zero line. Conversely, when momentum is positive, it will be above the line.

I know that all may sound confusing but what you get is a pattern showing the momentum of the stock. That information, of course, can be very important to our timing!

The most commonly used signal that the MACD provides is known as the "crossover signal." This occurs when the MACD line crosses *above* the Signal line. That is a positive signal. It becomes a negative signal when the MACD line crosses *below* the signal line. I like this signal quite a bit with one major caveat: The crossover must be in the same direction as the dominant price trend.

Microsoft was a company that I liked a great deal fundamentally, and it was also hard to ignore the strength of its uptrend on the charts. The MACD provided many bullish crossover signals along the way, as you can see on this chart:

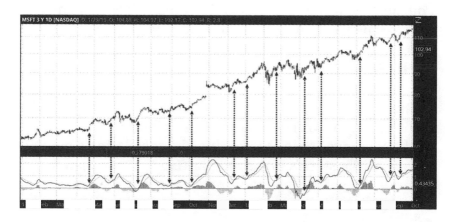

Certainly, not every crossover signal produced a windfall, but by and large, the signals did develop at junctures that represented good entry points in this strongly-trending and strongly-performing stock.

Another way to utilize the MACD is by focusing on the Histogram. It can often show us that things are potentially improving prior to the price improving. I keep an eye out for that type of development in stocks that I'm on the verge of acquiring. Intel's chart has a fine example where it paid to watch the Histogram develop:

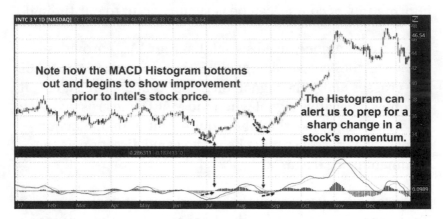

The value of the Histogram as a visual aid is undeniable. It's tipped me off to subsurface improvement in the momentum of a stock more times than I can remember. I don't initiate a buy just using the Histogram. However, it does help me to prepare my plan to purchase the shares in advance.

BOLLINGER BANDS®

Bollinger Bands® act like an envelope since they're plotted in such a way as to create an upper and lower "limit" to stock prices over time. This is done by calculating a moving average of the stock's price and plotting it. They then compute the volatility of the stock price over the same period of time. Using some fancy math, that we don't need to worry about here, they create upper and lower markers, or bands, forming an "envelope." When volatility increases, the bands will widen and during less volatile periods, they'll contract.

Another way to think about Bollinger Bands® is to visualize them as guardrails on a roadway. We know instinctively that if we veer too far to one side of the road or the other, we are approaching a dangerous area and we need to return to safety between the lines.

Bollinger Bands® can be used in many ways but one way to use them is to recognize when to be patient in acquiring a stock. If you come across a stock where the price is already outside the Bollinger Bands® it represents a situation where it's stretched from its trend. A visual will help me illustrate the form of Bollinger Bands® and highlight the need for *patience* they can provide.

Note that after popping above the upper band of the envelope, Microsoft either paused or pulled back.

This can help in deciding when to buy. Without the Bollinger Bands®, the action represented on the chart would look like a positive, upward trend and that's something we want to get in on. But by looking at the chart with the Bollinger Bands®, we might see that the price just broke through the upper band and is about to pull back. With a bit of patience, we'll get a better price.

Without Bollinger Bands®, the risk of entering a position when the stock's price is over-extended in the short-run becomes a real possibility. Bollinger Bands® can help us determine if we've arrived on the scene after a stock's price has become too stretched. We may want to let the stock take a "breather" (and let the price come back inside the Bands before acting).

MONEY-FLOW INDEX (MFI)

Money-flow is a specific technical indicator and also a category name for indicators that indicate whether money is flowing in or out of a stock over a certain period of time.

There are a number of indicators that you might choose. I prefer the Money-Flow Index (MFI). I like the way it's constructed, and it's served me well in different types of markets over the years.

Money-flow indicators typically focus on the stock price action in relation to trading volume. They look for clues to future direction based on the trend of those two factors. It's generally thought that if money is flowing into a stock it's positive, and it's negative if money is flowing out of a stock.

If MFI readings are rising, then positive price action is expected for the stock price. And if the MFI is falling, then expectations would be negative for the stock price.

In other words, MFI is thought to lead the price action.

I don't want to get too deep into the weeds as far as MFI math goes, but a way to think about it would be that it keeps a running total of the number of shares that were, theoretically, bought or sold over the course of a specific period of time. This would tell us whether investors are adding shares to their holdings or subtracting them.

Wall Street's operators can be pretty slick at times and they'll often use strength in a stock's price to sell shares and they'll use weakness to accumulate shares.

We can use the MFI to spot divergences between what the stock price is currently doing and what the cumulative flow of money *expects* the stock price to do in the future.

Apple (AAPL) had a few extremely interesting and potentially lucrative divergences in 2018. We'll look at a positive one first. In the following chart, note that the MFI line is shown in the bottom section while stock prices are indicated in the top section. See how the price was dropping while the MFI was trending upward?

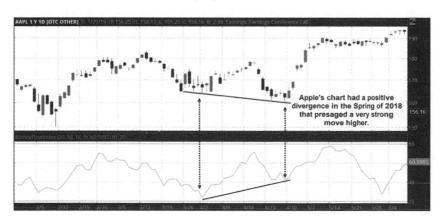

Apple's chart had a positive divergence in the Spring of 2018 that presaged a very strong move higher.

The stock price may have been lower in late April 2018 than early that month, but the MFI suggested that money was flowing into Apple quite strongly. The ensuing rally was extremely powerful.

On the flip side, and regrettably for Apple shareholders, there's no better recent example of a negative divergence like one that appeared in Apple in the Fall of 2018. See how strongly the MFI indicated a downward move even while the stock price was maintaining value? Eventually the stock did a significant reversal to indicate that the MFI was an accurate indicator of what the price was about to do.

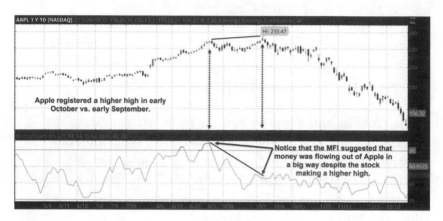

I strongly prefer to see the MFI confirm the stock's price action. If a stock is rising, I want to see money being committed to it. If the MFI is diverging greatly from the price action, as it did in Apple, that gets my attention, for sure. I've seen this type of price action too many times after the big money has moved out of a formerly solid stock. The outcomes can often be devastating.

Using MFIs is a way to get a peek into the future. It's not absolute and it isn't foolproof, but it has a solid track record and one that I use often. This is one that I suggest you take a look at and practice with for a while. It can be worth your time.

NOW YOU KNOW

Having knowledge is never a bad thing. Being paralyzed by inaction is a bad thing. I've given you these tools to help you refine your ability to recognize trends and maximize your potential towards Unstoppable Prosperity.

NOW EXECUTE

Pick one of these methods that you haven't used in the past and apply it to a hypothetical situation. Use one of the stocks in your portfolio and take a historical look at the time you made the buy. Did you pick a good time, or would this method have helped you refine your timing? If there was a better time, don't worry. Use the experience to learn as you move forward.

If it was good timing, good for you. Did the method you chose help you see why it was a good time to enter?

You can also do this assignment with your Watch List. There's a grand slam out there somewhere just waiting for the smart investor to find it. It's time for you to be that investor!

CHAPTER TEN

PUTTING IT ALL TOGETHER

Throughout the book you've seen how I approach investing. My Three Pillars have been exceptionally successful for me and now you have the opportunity to employ those same principles. I want to take some time to do a quick review.

Finding opportunities can be just a matter of being observant and asking questions. You can certainly watch financial television, read financial journals and listen to as many experts as you have the time to absorb. There's nothing wrong with that. The more information coming in, the more opportunities become available. But I never want you to discount your own knowledge, your own experiences or those of the people you come in contact with each day.

Tremendous opportunities can be found BEFORE the experts through paying attention to the world around you. Don't be afraid of being in front of the hot new trends. Just because the "experts" aren't recommending it yet doesn't mean it isn't a moneymaker. Trust in your research to separate the wheat from the chaff. Check out new companies. Look into new trends. Be aggressive. Just be sure to do the work before putting out the cash!

With that in mind, let's review my Three Pillars.

PILLAR 1 - FUNDAMENTAL ANALYSIS

Remember that fundamentals are crucial to any successful investment. The longer you intend to hold a particular position, the more they matter. The longer you intend to hold a stock the deeper you should dive to investigate those fundamentals.

I'm sure there'll be times where using the quick analysis strategies I outlined in Chapters 2 and 3 may be enough but I also know that doing a more extensive examination, including things like Peer-to-Peer reviews is never a waste of time.

There have been a number of times where I was convinced that a company was a solid investment after doing the quick analysis but as I got deeper into the evaluation I discovered information that let me know that either the company had issues that weren't immediately apparent or that there were other companies, competitors, that might be better choices for my money.

Doing the work, taking the time to research, is the first, and most basic step towards Unstoppable Prosperity. I cannot emphasize this enough - THERE ARE NO SHORTCUTS!

Okay, by now I know you understand how vital fundamentals are and how to go about identifying the key elements of those fundamentals. It isn't possible to do too much research. The more you know the better your successes will be.

PILLAR 2 - TECHNICAL ANALYSIS

If you're new to the market, or new to controlling your own investments, technicals can be intimidating. Charts can look confusing and there are so many things to look at. How are you supposed to master all of that? Well, to be a smart investor, you don't have to master them all. But you do have to be able to use some of them effectively. Being able to use charts effectively can be the difference between making a small profit and a large one, or the difference between a small loss and a backbreaking one. Being able to recognize patterns and extrapolate movement from those patterns provides an advantage to any investor willing to take the time to learn them and use them regularly.

This doesn't mean that you have to give up your day job and devote the next three years of your life to studying charts. It does mean that you need to spend some time studying and using the chart patterns and indicators you learned about. Choose the ones that you're most comfortable with, understand the information they provide, and use that information as you make decisions. Over time you'll get more and more comfortable with charts and how to use them. You can then add additional techniques to your knowledge base, making you that much more refined in your investment decisions.

Charts are tools. They're tools that will help you know when to enter or exit a position. They demonstrate patterns, which you can use to anticipate future events. They're not some secret that only experts can master, although some "experts" would like you to believe so. The more you can use charts, the more effective you can be.

PILLAR 3 - BEHAVIORAL ANALYSIS

Emotions are a fact of human nature. We might like to believe that we're always rational but that is just an illusion. The more important something is to us the more we have to be aware of how emotions might be impacting how we act. You already know how to read the emotions of others, you've been doing it since you were a child. If you have to deliver news to someone, you have a pretty good idea of how they'll react. Understanding the market requires that you do the same thing.

I mentioned the "herd mentality" earlier. This emotional response can drive stock prices up or down based on little or no information. Humans have an inherent need to avoid pain of any kind. The emotional pain of "missing out" or of "losing" or of "feeling foolish" can drive actions that might be contrary to our financial interests. It might seem that when talking about money or financial security, people would always be rational. The wild swings that sometimes occur in the market belie that belief!

There's no way to prevent others from reacting, or overreacting, emotionally. Nor can we eliminate our own emotional responses. The best we can do is not allow those responses to make judgements. Being aware that you're vulnerable, that you'll FEEL the same emotional tugs as those rushing to buy or sell because of a rumor, is vital. It's the best defense against making mistakes that can cost you dearly.

Be aware that people will always react emotionally and that swings in the market can be triggered or worsened by those reactions.

Recognize that while a turn in the market can be emotionally driven, it can also impact your portfolio. I'm not suggesting that you ignore the impact of the emotions of others, but rather that you make your decisions on logic. If logic tells you that you need to exit a position, for reasons that you understand and not a "gut" reaction, then do that. If a stock has taken off like a moonshot but there's been no basic change in the fundamentals, know that emotion is driving up the price and don't be foolish enough to chase it on that rise. You should now know that stocks that shoot up like that often fall back just the same way.

All three of my Pillars should have a vital role in your market decisions. I suggested earlier in the book that if you're looking at a position as a short-term trade, Technicals have to take the most important position. On the other hand, if long-term investment is your goal for a position fundamentals become foremost. In either case, an awareness of the emotions that might surround that position will help you determine the value to you and will allow you to make the best decisions based on your goals.

REMINDERS

Over time companies grow through organic innovation and through acquisitions, which means a company you previously lost money investing in may not be the same company today. Check back from time to time. Don't be afraid to move back into a company if you find that the fundamental proposition has changed and that the stock is moving in a positive, sustainable way. Refusing to revisit stocks just because it didn't work out the first time is about ego and emotion, not smart investing.

Also remember that hot stocks can often outstrip the reality of what they're offering. Hype drives prices far too often. To ignore this hype is a real threat to your sustainable wealth building. You can treat these high-flyers with a trading mentality or put them on your Watch List and wait for the reality to catch up with the hype for a longer-term investment. Just don't confuse the two.

So, we have our list and we have companies we simply keep an eye on. We have companies that come back into our orbit for a number of reasons, like seeing them on a list of daily movers or an article about them or their products. However a company creates interest, as a new company or one that has resurfaced, we have to follow the same careful steps and apply all my Pillars before spending our money.

Finally, I've said it repeatedly but feel like I need to say it once more – *have the right plan and stick to that plan.* Investing doesn't have to be gambling. Luck is great when it strikes but it's not going to make you a successful investor.

Planning, execution and discipline are the keys to achieving your goals.

I want you to achieve your goals.

But to do that you MUST know the plan and stick to the plan. This is your roadmap. When you face circumstances for the first time or just aren't sure what you need to do next, I want you to do two things:

1. **Review your plan** - How does a decision you make get you closer to achieving the goals of that plan?

2. **Review this book** - Review the section(s) that applies to your situation at that time. Never assume that you have to be an expert or that you "know it all." That kind of thinking leads to overconfidence and mistakes.

People are surprised when I tell them I consider myself to still be a student of the market. I'm learning every day. I want you to have that same thirst for knowledge. That's how you continuously become a better, more profitable investor.

You have the tools and you've demonstrated the drive to

accomplish your dreams. You can succeed with this.

Think about other areas in your life where you've had success. It's not some elusive impracticable thing. It's actually a fairly predictable process.

Regardless of what you're trying to succeed at, it takes many of the same elements. It requires a strong desire for a specific outcome. Then learning the fundamentals, committing to a pattern that reinforces, refines and ultimately masters those fundamentals and develops the skills necessary to get the result.

It's no different here.

You simply need to make the decision it's worth the time to do those things with what I've taught you throughout this book.

One of my great frustrations are the multitude of people that believe that fate in life was decided at birth or they can't overcome their current circumstances.

No one would have looked at a 12-year-old Charles, sitting on a Greyhound bus with his mother and two brothers, heading to the mean streets of Harlem, penniless and afraid, and thought, "There's someone who's destined for success."

From the stand point of circumstance, I faced too many obstacles that had devoured so many lives and dreams. What I did have going for me, were the ingredients that I mentioned earlier. I never felt my situation and place in life were permanent.

I was determined to change my fate and that determination created a thirst for knowledge and a willingness to work hard.

You can do this.

You can have Unstoppable Prosperity regardless of your current circumstances, if, you'll do the work. And believe me when I tell you, it's a much smaller price than the price of doing nothing.

I realize that some of you, heck maybe even most of you, are sitting there right now excited about the prospects of being able to create Unstoppable Prosperity, but you're not sure you know everything you need to know to pull it off.

You may have some fear and trepidation. Well, let me clear that up. You're right! You don't know everything you need to know. Much of what you need to understand only comes while you're working at it. That's how it always is. You really only begin to understand things when you're moving forward and trying to execute. Uncertainty in the beginning is normal. Don't let it stop you from getting started.

Think back to the first time you sat behind the wheel of a car. Do you remember the feelings of excitement? Do you remember how they were mixed with the fear that you might mess this up and get yourself (and anyone with you) killed?

Oh, the freedom that awaited you! And, the pit in the bottom of your stomach! Were either of those feelings unfounded? No, of course not. Learning to drive did ultimately lead to the freedom you anticipated. But, at the same time, there was a very real possibility that the worst could happen too.

Taking control of your financial future isn't unlike that. It does hold the promise of freedom from the fear of running out of money and the burden of having to grind every day into the twilight of life. More importantly, it holds the promise of making dreams of those around you come true and your golden years golden.

But on the other side of that fence is the potential to make mistakes and crash on the way to that freedom. But just like it was worth the risk to perfect the art of driving a car, it's worth the risk of taking control of this critical piece of your wealth equation.

Now, if you're like most people, you probably didn't steal your parent's vehicle and learn to drive all by yourself on some dark street. You probably had someone sitting next to you to guide and reassure you. In fact, in many cases there was someone sitting next to you with a brake on their side of the vehicle – just in case you lost control. You can't overstate the value in that. It eased your fears and protected you from yourself. This kind of support is valuable any time you're learning something new, or even if you're trying to get better at something you already do.

I'm totally committed to helping anyone who has the desire and the drive to create Unstoppable Prosperity accomplish that goal. I didn't write this book for me. My life is pretty good. I wrote this book to give back and give a hand up to anyone who has the desire to significantly change their financial picture. I'm committed to that, and I want to give you all the help you need to increase the odds that you can pull this off.

I've done my best to detail out for you exactly what I did to create Unstoppable Prosperity for me and my family starting with nothing. Some of you will be able to take what I've given you in this book and, combined with your own determination, be able to accomplish it for yourself. But others of you may require some personal guidance and more specific information.

Sometimes, when it comes down to executing, you need very specific information that applies to a very specific situation. That can only happen in an exchange between you and someone who knows how to do this well. Since I know that, I've put together a team of people who can have that back and forth with you. And if necessary, who can sit in the seat next to you long enough to make sure you understand my approach and know how to execute well.

Now, I don't know which of you will need that extra support… you may not even know yourself at this point. So, I'd love to give you the opportunity to at least have a conversation with a member of my team, so we can get to know you. Once we know you and your situation, we can determine together what, if any, additional help you may need to give you the greatest odds of succeeding.

I'm serious about this and will do everything in my power to give you a hand up and help you hit the ground running.

For those of you who have decided now is the time for you to get serious about creating Unstoppable Prosperity, the next step is to reach out and schedule a one on one conversation with a member of my team. Once we understand your unique situation, we'll be in a position to steer you in the right direction.

*Go to **www.PaynesTeam.com** or call us at **1-800-296-9890***

Procrastination is the biggest killer to success, don't allow that here. Make the decision, don't set this aside telling yourself you'll get started sometime in the future. If you do nothing, your excitement about this will naturally diminish, usually pretty rapidly. So, call right now and at least get an appointment scheduled. Put it on the calendar so you're more likely to get rolling, and then we'll join you for the ride until you get it figured out.

I've said this a couple times already, but I want to say it again - **you can do this**. Think about how you feel about driving now. The challenges are there but the fear isn't like it used to be.

Would you like to put fear in the rearview mirror when it comes to investing?

Would you like to go down the road of life with the right map and tools to reach you best destination?

Once you master these techniques you'll own a skill set that is hard to place a value on. Moments that would have called for panic in the past are now seen as opportunities.

Imagine never having to be in a position where you stop accumulating knowledge and wealth.

Reach out to my team and let's get after this... Unstoppable Prosperity awaits.

~ Charles Payne